GETTING EVEN

HANDLING CONFLICT
so that
BOTH SIDES WIN

*John W. Vale and
Robert B. Hughes*

PYRANEE
BOOKS

Zondervan Publishing House
Grand Rapids, Michigan

Getting Even: Handling Conflict So That Both Sides Win

This is a Pyranee Book
Published by the Zondervan Publishing House,
1415 Lake Drive, S.E., Grand Rapids, Michigan 49506

Library of Congress Cataloging in Publication Data

Vale, John W.
  Getting even.

  "A Pyranee book"—T.p. verso.
    1. Conflict management—Religious aspects—Christianity. 2. Church contro-
versies. I. Hughes, Robert B., 1946– II. Title.
BV4525.V34   1987   248.4   87-8108
ISBN 0-310-35661-X

Edited and designed by David Lambert

Printed in the United States of America

87 88 89 90 91 / EE / 10 9 8 7 6 5 4 3 2 1

To our wives,
Dianna Vale and Susan Hughes

CONTENTS

75637

INTRODUCTION

When God forgave our sins against him, he demonstrated a powerful way for us to deal with sins against us—a way too often ignored when we find ourselves knee-deep in arguments and disputes: the way of forgiveness. And forgiveness is not the responsibility of Jesus alone—it is the ongoing obligation of every Christian. That's easy to say and hard to do. Why? Because all too often we want to fight, not forgive.

All of us have thrown our stones of hate or murmured our whispers of gossip. We all have had conflicts. But I have never met a person who would not prefer to settle those conflicts and live in peace. We fight on the outside and crave peace and forgiveness on the inside.

As the population grows, so do the problems. To solve them, we need to develop our peace-making skills. And resolving our conflicts begins with ourselves. We trust, therefore, that you will take the practical knowledge you gain from this book and use it in your own daily Christian life. It is our hope that *Getting Even* will be a help and inspiration in resolving your conflicts, past, present, or future.

John W. Vale
Robert B. Hughes

PART I

WHAT IS CONFLICT, AND HOW DO WE HANDLE IT?

Do not repay evil with evil or insult
with insult, but with blessing, because
to this you were called so that you
may inherit a blessing (1 Peter 3:9).

CHAPTER 1
HOW DO WE
HANDLE CONFLICT?

*Conflict is a fact of life. We can't avoid it—
we can only learn from it. In the heat of the
moment, we usually want conflict resolved our
own way, and we forget to be sensitive to
other points of view, especially God's. And
sometimes we're afraid to admit that we even
have conflicts; still, sharing those conflicts
opens the door to dispelling fear and releasing
forgiveness—the two keys to resolving conflict.*

CONFLICT IS A FACT OF LIFE

Never the Same Again

Christmas was just around the corner. Don and Ellen Andrews and their eighteen-year-old son James had begun talking over their holiday plans—which was good, because lately they hadn't been talking much about anything.

Don and Ellen's recent separation had eased the tensions at home; a friend's mediation had also helped. It was true that James hadn't been around home much lately, but maybe the holidays could help take the chill off their relationship. So far, their family problems had been kept reasonably quiet from relatives and friends; maybe they could get through all of this without major trauma.

One night, as Don and Ellen slept in their separate homes, their son James acted out the frustration and guilt that had been building inside him for many years.

The next day Mr. and Mrs. Downing, the Andrews's neighbors, read the morning paper.

—"Oh, no. Don Andrews? That was *his* son who tried to kill a policeman and got shot several times?"

—"Yes, and they were such a nice family, although I think they've been separated for awhile. James seems like such a nice boy. Why would he do such a thing?"

—"I don't know. Who really knows what's going on inside a person's head? One thing for sure—things will never be the same for them again."

That's right—never the same again. Now James faces the pain of operations and recuperation, a trial, a probable jail sentence, as well as a shattered reputation in the church and community. He has become a family disgrace.

The Andrews's family failures, once hidden, now have been plastered on the front page of the newspaper. The entire family must face friends and relatives—some who will understand, some who will be shocked, some who will blame, and some who will forgive. What will they say? What will they think? The Andrews were a prominent Christian family in the community—what about their Christian testimony? Should they move to another state? How can they put their lives back together again? Now it seems that the whole world knows of the failures of father, mother, and son.

Things will never be the same again.

And why should they be? Things were terrible the way they were. Why should the Andrews go on in their destructive lifestyle? One by one they laid the bricks of conflict and mortared them with pride. Don and Ellen always were crabbing at each other, and James often was caught in the middle—loving and hating each parent at the same time. His determination to continue his schooling and to move on in his life had shriveled.

Even when Don and Ellen learned of the shooting, they immediately blamed each other.

—"If you had only been more of a father, this would
  have never happened!"

—"If you hadn't put your career over your son, he
  would've stayed at home instead of out on the
  streets!"

They heaped blame upon blame, while their son lay bleeding in an emergency room. Of course things can never be the same again. But they can be better.

Destruction or Reconciliation?

The Andrews face a fork in the road—the same we all face when we are in conflict. We can choose to stay ruined, or we can choose to rebuild. The neighbors who spoke over morning coffee probably did not see the second choice. All they saw was the tragedy, the hole the Andrews had dug for themselves. They doomed the Andrews to bear the stigma and live in the shadows of their failures. After all, how can deep marital failure and criminal behavior ever really be forgotten?

This is a book about that kind of forgetting, about solving problems without blaming others and giving ourselves a life sentence in the prison of our conflicts and failures. The Andrews didn't start out their lives planning to fall into such gut-wrenching conflict, but they found themselves right in the middle of it. What will their next move be? More conflict-creating behavior? Or will they forgive, reconcile, and forget?

Their lives will go on, either in ruins or in rebuilding. Choosing to go on with forgiveness will not make the consequences of their conflicts or the depths of their pain go away, but it will ensure that their future will be better than their past.

The Andrews' family conflicts were often fueled by the burning thought, "I'll get even if it's the last thing I do." Get even! That thought also can be the unspoken and subconscious driving force behind our own behavior during a conflict. We do need to get even, but we need to get even in a positive sense, not by lashing out in hurt and bitterness but by finding solutions that will give justice and dignity to both sides. Conflict is a fact of life, but knowing how to get even so that *both* sides win is something we all need.

Constant Conflicts

We may never face the kind of conflicts the Andrews faced, but from the time we wake up each morning, we face hundreds of conflicts and decisions. Will we get up or sleep a little more? We may want to sleep some more, but we also have a churning need to get going. Even though this is a minor decision, it creates within us a conflict that will need to be resolved.

And so our days go—one potential conflict after another. Big ones and little ones. Some demand a small amount of our thoughts and emotions; others make our stomachs churn. Each decision affects the rest of our day. For example, if we decide to stay in bed all day, we will get the rest we crave— but we also might get fired from our job.

If you could sit down and plan an ideal day, what would you include? You probably wouldn't program in fights with your spouse or neighbors, flat tires in the middle of traffic jams, or howling cats outside your window for half the night. Who wants conflict? Struggling, fighting, and hurting are aspects of life we would just as soon live without. A perfect day would be one without conflict—and we know too well that perfect days do not exist.

Like it or not, conflict is not an option on the dashboard of life—it is standard equipment. It's also automatic; it's on whenever the machine is running. We can try to ignore conflict, but its red warning light eventually gets our attention. We have to deal with it or suffer a breakdown.

It is our nature to deny problems and hope they will go away. They seldom do. Though hidden for a short time, at some point they emerge again; often more severely than before, as in the case of the Andrews family.

Whether our conflicts are large or small, we have to face and resolve them every day of our lives. Where will we go? What will we buy? What should we say? Minor conflicts are no problem except for one complication—we make mistakes. If we always made correct choices, our minor conflicts would only amount to the spice of life that keeps us alert and faced with healthy challenge. Because we make wrong, late, or no decisions, minor conflicts can turn into raging fires that can destroy healthy thinking.

It is time for us to stop hiding from our conflicts and admit two things: 1) *we make mistakes,* and 2) *we can work through problems and move to a better life.*

THE RISKS OF RUNNING FROM CONFLICT

Is there anyone left who really thinks Christians never have disputes and conflicts? The church seemed to teach that in years past, and some people really seemed to believe it. But by now, we've all learned the truth: *church people have problems.* And what makes those problems worse is the attempt to cover up and ignore them rather than to face them. Denial delays resolution.

Hiding Increases Guilt

Bill cheated on his taxes many years ago. For years he knew he should pay those back taxes. Though time passed, his guilt did not. When Bill's conscience could no longer cover his mistake, he finally confessed his wrong and paid the taxes. Some members of his church approved; others disapproved. Some were surprised that such a good Christian would ever do a thing like that. Bill, however, had to bring his conflict into the open in order to resolve his guilt. So do we.

Hiding Breeds Despair

How would you respond to the following situations?

Your church is split down the middle over whether or not you should start a new building project. Many feel that you should not talk about the conflict because Christians should not have those kind of problems. Do you deny the conflict and hide the issue?

You feel uncomfortable about telling someone that you have a marital problem. Your spouse is bringing a lawsuit. Even though it is not your fault, you feel that you just cannot tell people about it because they may not understand or they may be too judgmental. Do you hide your need for counsel?

A member of your church hit your car, and now you have insurance problems. The two of you cannot agree how to best handle a complicated and many-sided issue. Do you ignore the disagreement and hope it resolves itself?

In these and other situations, we often prefer to *deny* conflict rather than *face* it. But that denial merely delays the resolution of the problem. We need to remember that *having* conflicts is not unspiritual—but *not dealing with them* is.

Every day we have the opportunity to resolve differences at home or work. Those differences usually don't involve hot anger and shouting matches. At issue are the little differences that can grow into deep-seated quarrels.

But some of us find it hard to accept the fact that Christians have even minor disputes. That idea doesn't come from the Bible; it comes from a theological fallacy—that once we are saved, we won't have any problems. The practical result of that fallacy is that when we fall into conflicts with others, we slide into quiet desperation and hiding. We think that no one must know we have problems. After all, we are supposed to be able to live above conflicts.

And in heaven we will. But it just doesn't work that way on earth.

When people come to us for counseling, they often apologize for their problems:

—"I know as Christians we shouldn't be having this kind of problem, but . . ."

—"My husband is really very kind, but he's so busy with his work that he has no time for me. I know we're not supposed to have problems like this, but . . ."

—"I hate to admit it, but I really resent my wife's social activities that take her away from the home. I know I shouldn't be this way, but . . ."

All humans—Christians included—have to admit to hard times and disturbed feelings. That's normal; it's not sinful. What we *do* with our feelings is the crucial step that will determine rightness or wrongness. We need to admit that we have problems before we can start to resolve and reconcile them.

This is especially important for parents. How do we parents resolve our conflicts? If we can't resolve our own problems, how can we teach our children to do it?

Frank considered himself to be a strong disciplinarian. When his two boys got into a fight over a toy, Frank would move in and solve the problem. He would take the toy away. "You two will see this again when you learn how to get along!"

When his boys argued over what to watch on TV, he applied his usual methods: "Go to your room until you can act right" or "OK! We'll watch what I want to watch."

Frank's solutions gave him the peace and quiet his tired ears needed, but they did nothing to teach his sons how to resolve their problems. What they learned from Frank was the place of power in resolving conflict. The strongest one wins by either banishing the troublemakers to another place or by overriding the weaker group's votes with a power vote of his own.

Where, in Frank's approach to problem solving, is the place for sitting down and talking things out? It's easy to try to solve problems by merely separating ourselves from the conflict. The toy went on the shelf, but the players learned nothing good about how to resolve their conflicts. Instead, they learned to deny the roots of their conflict, hide from discussing the problem, and cover it all up with a change of scenery or activity.

Let's admit it: In the real world, we live with internal and external conflict. Though the conflict itself may not be sin, how we handle it could lead us into sin. That is why this book was written—to show that conflicts can be resolved to the glory of God.

Hiding Can Destroy Relationships

How many times have you walked into a room, spoken a few words, and before you knew it, someone is upset with you? You try to muzzle your anger and maintain a pleasant exterior. Later you wrestle with bad feelings about yourself and about the other person. Maybe you'll eventually forget about the minor flare-up. Or it could become kindling for a big burn-up later on.

We are afraid to confront. Many of us have been involved in one of the more cosmic conflicts of this age: the-neighbor's-dog-did-where-he-shouldn't dispute. At first, we thought our patience was admirable. We noticed the deposits several times and cleaned them up, thinking to ourselves, "Why don't they make the beast go on *their* lawn!" We even considered saying something to our neighbor. Should we march over there right now? No, better cool off first. Besides, we need to come up with just the right words—something like, "Nice day isn't it? Too bad I have to spend it cleaning up your dog's messes."

After struggling with the problem, we realize that it's easier just to live with it and to clean up the mess. But the irritation festers into bitterness.

If we cannot bring ourselves to talk to the people we have problems with, we probably will manage to talk to everyone else. It seems we can talk easily to someone who is not involved, but we find it almost impossible to talk to the person who is involved. Spreading our tales of woe gives the impression that we are dealing openly with our problems. But the impression is just a smoke screen that conceals our unwillingness to be open with the only person who matters: the one with whom we have the conflict.

We are afraid to take action. For several years Tom and Jim argued about the fence between their yards. Neither wanted to take the responsibility for fixing the deteriorating boards. Rather than discussing the problem openly, they began to shy away from the problem and from each other as much as possible. With frustration and bad feelings building between them, they soon stopped talking to each other.

Finally, things became so intolerable that Tom decided he had to talk about it with Jim. His worst fears were realized: Jim was hostile and angry. Convinced more than ever that his neighbor was both irresponsible and unreasonable, Tom went back home and hired a fence company to tear down the old fence and build a new one so high that he wouldn't have to see his neighbor.

Tom and Jim could have done many things that would have altered the outcome:

—They could have talked it over early, rather than letting it build until it exploded.

—They could have fixed the old fence long before it deteriorated.

—They could have agreed to have a fence party and fix it together.

Anything would have been better than what they did— deny the conflict and let it fester.

Avoiding conflict is as great a threat to a good relationship as is open hostility. Hiding disagreement only turns up the heat under the pressure cooker of conflict. The inevitable explosion probably will be greater, increasing the pain and deepening the wound. Start working on conflict early, when the relationship has not been damaged.

How Do We Respond to Conflict?

When faced with a conflict, are we hiders or fighters? Either way, one thing controls our response more than we would like to admit: *our desire to get our own way.*

If we think we can get our own way, we stay and fight for it. If not, we run away. Either way, we see only our side of the conflict. But more sides are involved—the other person's perspective and God's perspective. And we are ready to resolve a conflict only when we understand all sides.

Dealing with all sides of a conflict can be difficult. Most

of us want to participate in decisions that affect us in positive ways, but few of us are willing to accept final settlements that don't go our way. It is not realistic to expect to win every conflict. If we want to solve a conflict, we are going to have to make concessions, be willing to put ourselves in the other person's shoes, and see how the conflict looks from the other side.

Probe for reasons. Several times recently Jay had come home late from work without calling his wife, Sally. When it happened again yesterday, Sally flew off the handle, took the kids, and went to her mother's for the night. She didn't take the time or make the effort to talk it out; she simply left with the children.

Was she right or wrong? Let's look at it from Jay's point of view:

She's being completely unfair. She didn't ask if I had even been *able* to call her yesterday. She shot first and asked questions later. It wasn't fair for her to conclude that I had no good reason for not calling. She always jumps the gun.

Now Sally gets equal time:

He's being completely unfair. Whatever reasons he may have had, he was being inconsiderate—as usual. Why should I have to put up with continual guesswork as to where he is and when he's coming home? He always forgets to think about anybody but himself. If he loved me, he'd share with me.

Why don't they both think about asking each other some questions rather than just opening up with both barrels? The only way to discover whether Sally's response was proper is for them to probe for the reasons behind Jay's actions and her response. And so they did—they began to ask each other questions, rather than just accepting the surface reasons for the conflict.

As they did, they began to see that their whole marriage was on shaky ground. Jay knew that he, like many men, didn't open up very much about himself—about his fears, desires, frustrations, or dreams. Sally said that that made her feel ignored and shut out. They also confirmed that Jay often worked late without telling Sally ahead of time. He didn't do it to frustrate her on purpose; it was just a habit he had fallen into. They came to see that the effect of that and other habits on their marriage was disastrous. Sally had taken it as long as she could—and then she blew.

Seeing the reasons behind their actions helped them see the best place to start in finding a solution: Jay needed to become more considerate! If they hadn't probed behind Sally's external blow-up, they could easily have misunderstood the real issues involved.

For another example, a friend is very upset with a sermon your pastor just preached and is considering leaving the church. Ask some probing questions before you tell your friend what a great guy the pastor is and how your friend must be mistaken in some way.

Why did the pastor preach that sermon? Did your friend talk to the pastor about it? Did the pastor do some other things that offended your friend? Try to look at the problem from both sides. What about the other members of the church, especially the ones who felt it was the best sermon they ever heard?

Look at the other person's point of view. Seeing only our own point of view is too easy. Work hard on trying to see how the other person might be seeing things. For example:

YOU	YOUR NEIGHBOR
I like to let them have their privacy.	They never ask how we are.
Their kids always play on our sidewalk.	We make sure our children stay off their lawn.
He always mows over on our side of the lawn.	I'll give him a head start on mowing his lawn.
Their house needs painting.	We don't have money for paint, but we keep the house neat and clean.
She intrudes on our privacy and time.	I want her to feel my interest and care.

Work hard to understand how the other person interprets his or her actions. There is always another point of view. Just because a particular interpretation occurs to you immediately, don't assume that it's the correct one.

Give up the mentality that instantly polarizes issues into *us versus them*. That polarization darkens a conflict with an all-or-nothing cloud that amounts to blackmail: "If I don't get it my way, we're through!" This "divorce mentality," of course, is graphically demonstrated in the marital disasters that surround us today, but it can just as easily be manifested toward business associates and friends.

Getting rid of the divorce mentality isn't easy; it's hard work to see beyond our own positions. It's also risky. It means we will have to do some sharing. How else will we come to understand the other person's side? How else will we receive good counsel to understand God's viewpoint?

Fear of Change

Suppose you do make an effort to see the conflict from the other person's point of view, and you discover that, in some ways, that person was right. Now you're obligated to make some changes in your own position, and nobody likes to do that. We want it *our* way. We like to think about resolving our conflicts, but we're upset if that solution doesn't include getting our way.

Recently I met a mother who was unhappy with her seventeen-year-old daughter's behavior. The daughter was staying out late, seeing a boy the mother disapproved of, and in general not paying attention to her mother's advice. The mother got upset with the daughter and ordered the daughter out of her home. It was all or nothing. No listening, no working things out. Change completely or leave.

Jackie was involved in a car wreck. Only minor damage was done to the other car, but the owner wouldn't talk to Jackie or her insurance company. He would only say, "I'll see you in court. Don't talk to me, talk to my attorney." His mind was made up. It would be all his way or nothing.

Confrontive, no-compromise attitudes like these only lead to dead ends. The purpose of this book is to teach constructive means of negotiating past those fears, past that anger, to a win-win solution.

SUMMARY

Conflict is a hard part of life. Sure, we would all love the easygoing approach to good times, but life is just not like that. This book will help us develop a healthy view of conflict. And it will help us work through conflicts, whether they are small or seemingly insurmountable.

We must learn to tap God's love and forgiveness and not let Satan blackmail us into fear, anger, and depression about unresolved conflicts. We will learn that sharing our conflicts with the right person will release us, not destroy us. Handling our conflicts correctly will break the power that tempts us to deny the conflict or to respond in anger and hostility.

"In your anger do not sin": Do not
let the sun go down while you are
still angry, and do not give the devil
a foothold (Ephesians 4:26–27).

CHAPTER 2
IS CONFLICT BAD?

*Actually, conflict can be either good or bad.
To a large degree it depends on what we
make of it. The desired goal of a dispute
should not be victory but peace.
Each conflict can be the beginning of the
solution to painful problems.*

FINDING A PERSONAL VIEW OF CONFLICT

It was not until Bill was arrested for drunken driving that Sharon realized he had a problem. Sure, the two of them would have a social drink now and then, but Sharon did not realize Bill was drinking regularly. One night, after Bill had had one too many, he drove through a red light and hit another car. Bill went to the hospital, and the driver of the other car went into eternity.

That trauma cracked open Bill's life for the first time. When Bill found himself in jail facing serious criminal charges, he could have chosen to see this as the end of life and hope. But he didn't. The enormous pain was the start of acknowledgment, acceptance, and healing. Conflict can be the painful lance that breaks open the boil and allows the healing to begin.

Frankly, until Bill's accident, Sharon really did not know too much about him. But during the months of hospitalization and court appearances, Sharon and Bill became very close. They needed each other more than ever before. Through this conflict their level of communication became deep and meaningful. Through the difficulty, they learned not only to face their problems but also how to deal with them constructively.

In this instance, conflict was the beginning of peace and wholeness for Bill and Sharon. Conflict can be a positive stress that can bring greater maturity and strength. Or conflict can bring greater immaturity and weakness.

Is conflict good or bad? This chapter deals with our personal perspectives and attitudes toward conflict. We must begin by asking ourselves personal and private questions:

—How well do I cope with conflicts?
—How willing am I to accept my own responsibility in a conflict?
—How clearly can I distinguish between opinion and fact?
—How willing am I to communicate openly with others?
—Do I assume the worst?

Conflict and the Garden of Eden

Conflict existed even before Adam and Eve sinned. It wasn't the kind of conflict we associate with anger, pain, or frustration. The conflict was a challenge, a set of problems that needed to be solved, a set of complex choices that needed to be made. It was a good kind of conflict, and it was present from the very start of creation, in the sinless serenity of the Garden of Eden.

God commanded Adam and Eve to come to grips with the entire earth. He told them to "fill the earth and subdue it. Rule over the fish of the sea and the birds of the air and over every living creature that moves on the ground" (Gen. 1:28). The first humans were called upon to build an ordered society that filled the earth. No easy task.

The Garden of Eden itself needed to be tilled and kept— a healthy and real challenge to humans. The tasks of cultivating the Garden and subduing the earth were not busywork. Adam and Eve could not just sit around and be fed and cared for while the world served their every whim. Their very well-being was dependent upon actively meeting the challenge of a vital and untamed world. If they did not "till and keep" the Garden, it would not properly produce necessary food. In fact that challenge was a blessing from God: "God blessed them and said . . ." (Gen. 1:28).

Another challenge that is more like the conflict we know today was the presence of the temptation to sin. That temptation was part of a sinless environment. The tilling and keeping of the Garden and the outward movement to subduing the entire earth was to take place in the face of satanic opposition—and all this before humans had complicated the matter by sinning and before God had enveloped the earth in His divine curse.

Taking a Second Look at Yourself

In our fallen world, healthy challenge is now shot through with frustrating toil. But we have the option of meeting our challenges in one of two ways—constructively or destructively. Conflict is not automatically bad. Its goodness or badness is determined by how we respond. Our attitude is the key to turning opposition into a positive experience.

Conflict often hurts, but that doesn't mean it is bad. We can learn from the Olympic show-jumping champion who had fallen off her horse hundreds of times. When she was just a little girl, her grandfather had told her that every time she fell off a horse, she would be a better rider when she got back on. So she never worried about falling off. Though that did not make her falls any less painful, her perspective on the pain gave her the insight and courage to use it for positive goals.

How we react to a conflict will greatly affect the process and the outcome. We need to develop a high personal responsibility for our own words and acts. We must know what we are saying and why we are saying it. Flying off the handle will feel great, but it will send a message to the other person that we are more interested in relieving our pent up hostilities than in being a responsible part of solving the problem.

Keep the Circle Small

One thing that makes a conflict bad is when the circle of people who know about the conflict expands to include those who have no part in its solution. When we are in the middle of conflicts, we need to be able to talk to people about the conflict, but we don't need the opinions of every relative and friend. It's important to discern who are the right people to talk to in a conflict situation.

Frank and Julia had conflict in their seventeen-year marriage and had asked for help in mediating their pending divorce. One of the major problems that had to be worked through was the erroneous advice that friends and relatives had given them:

— "My friend went through the same thing! What you've got to watch out for is the way he'll try to get as much as he can without giving you your share."

— "Lawyers are all alike; they're just in it for the money. Make sure you get one that will really pull for your end of the bargain."

— "Christians should not take each other to court, so you and Julia really ought to avoid all litigation. Work things out yourselves."

— "Just love her and everything will be all right."

— "Don't move out; make her move."

— "Fight tooth and nail for the children."

— "Don't put up with it any more. He'll never change; my Sam didn't."

With that kind of advice, it was no wonder they were confused and were seeking a divorce.

After several mediation sessions and many hours of

research, they were shown that most of their so-called good advice was false and did not relate to their specific problems. One by one, Frank and Julia worked through their problems and the end result was positive.

The couple still has problems to work out, but instead of giving up and making unreasonable demands of each other, they are talking to each other in a spirit of compromise and understanding. Though the friends meant well, their interest was not in mending the problem; it was one of meddling where they did not belong.

PASSIVITY OR PEACEMAKING?

Letting God Handle It

Conflicts are good if we see them as opportunities to let God show His power. However, we must be careful when we say we're going to let God handle the problem. It's easy for some of us to be passive—to just sit and let whatever happens happen. We might say, "I've turned the problem over to God, so I've done all I have to do." Turning the problem over to God is indeed an important first step, but God desires a bit more participation than just that act of faith. He desires us to make peace. Turning it over to the Lord is only the first step. How we act and what we do *after* we turn it over to God will decide the outcome. God acts through us. We are His messengers. We are peacemakers, not adversaries, in a dispute.

One afternoon my neighbor, Jim, told me about some trouble he was having with the paperboy. Apparently the paperboy often missed his porch, and some days he forgot to deliver Jim's paper altogether. Jim was fed up and was ready to cancel his subscription. "I've prayed about this problem, but it seems as if God doesn't really care. He hasn't done a thing about it."

"Maybe God wants you to do more than pray about the situation. Maybe He wants you to talk to the paperboy," I suggested.

Several weeks later, we were outside talking again when Jim said, "Oh, by the way, you'll never guess what happened. I called the paperboy and he was very apologetic, came right over with a paperbox, and every day the paper is dry and in the box." Jim chuckled and said, "I guess God wanted me to be part of the solution to my own problem."

Work Side By Side, Not Head On

Disputing also will be less painful if we can learn to treat our opponent as a partner. Rather than seeing the other person as an adversary, see him or her as a co-worker, both of you working together to reach a fair settlement.

After all, in any dispute, both sides are 100 percent responsible until a resolution is found. It is like borrowing money from the bank. If you and I go to a bank and jointly borrow $500.00, each of us has to sign the note and each is 100 percent responsible until the note is paid off.

The same principle applies to a dispute. If you and I are involved, we cannot just walk away from it. We are equal partners until the dispute is settled. As peacemakers, we must assume full responsibility for the resolution of the problem.

What if we did not want to get into the conflict? What if we had no responsibility for causing the problem in the first place? Though that may be true, it misses the point. We need to separate responsibility for solving the problem from responsibility for causing the problem. Once that is done, we will be freed up to work as partners. We may have no responsibility for causing the problem, but we have full responsibility for seeing it through to resolution. To cease the quest for reconciliation is to cease being a peacemaker.

God did not cause the problem of sin, but He fully involved Himself as peacemaker until the problem was solved in Christ's sacrifice and resurrection. Regardless of how difficult our own problems or disputes are, we will be better able to work out a friendly reconciliation of the problem once we accept the idea that we both have a problem and must share and face it together as allies, not enemies.

And that's nearly impossible to do unless we learn to *separate the person from the problem.* We tend to view conflicts as face-to-face confrontations, and we see the other person in the conflict as our adversary. In that context, anything either of us says about the problem will be taken personally and will make it difficult to get down to the real problem and resolution. To be a peacemaker is to be neither passive nor aggressive. How can disputing be bad if two peacemakers are working together?

CHOOSE YOUR WORDS CAREFULLY

Sometimes conflict becomes bad when we use it to lash out at the other person. Under the guise of being open with our feelings, we often attack the other person: "You always react that way"; or "You never try to work things out"; or "You always blow your stack. Can't you settle down?" or "You're just being selfish."

These statements are all too easy to make, especially when we are upset. They convey hostility and assure a bad dispute. The response we will get to those words is usually defensive or offensive, and the solution to our problem gets buried even more deeply.

Talk in the First Person

We can turn a bad conflict around if we let our comments reveal how we are being affected by the discussion rather than making a judgment on the other person. Speaking in terms of ourselves, not the other, helps diffuse hostility and eventually reveals what the problem is.

Learn to say: "When you do that, I feel hurt"; or "When you react that way, I think that you are angry with me"; or "When you stop working on the problem, I feel frustrated and don't know how to go on"; or "When you respond that way, I feel like doing the same. I need a calmer climate in order to work this out"; or "When you seek your own interests, I am at a loss about how I can have some of my needs met."

The point is to tell the other person how his or her behavior affects us. Instead of saying, "You're talking too fast," try, "I am having trouble understanding you." Conversing in this manner will help us avoid judging the other person, increasing his or her feelings of being under attack.

Parents and children can turn pesky points of irritation into relationship-deepening times of mutual sharing. Instead of nagging, "Why do you always leave your clothes all over the floor!" a mother can say, "When I find your clothes on the floor, I feel as if you don't care about me. I feel like your slave, not your mother." And instead of shouting, "Don't you smart-mouth me, boy!" a father can say, "When you talk to me like that, I feel as if you have no love or respect for me. Have I wronged you in some way?"

Using ourselves as examples is also less confrontational to the other person. We do not have to make ourselves the reference point for everything, but we focus on our reaction rather than the other person's actions. This will help clear the way for a solution.

There is, though, one danger in talking in the first person. If we're not careful, we can sound like a know-it-all. That's particularly true if we use statements like: "I did it this way," or "This happened to me." We should feel free to use examples from our past or from people close to us, but we must be careful not to give the impression that we know something about everything or that we can always go one better than the other person. Let our true stories come out only if they can be helpful to the problem at hand. Being a know-it-all can turn a good discussion sour. If in doubt, say nothing.

Emphasize the Positive

A conflict can become bad if we allow negativism to cloud the relationship. A long-time business partnership failed when the two partners gradually reached the point that they could no longer communicate constructively. How did the problem start? It started with little comments. When one of the partners showed up late for work, the other assumed the worst and made some comment about not caring about the business. When one of them showed up late for an appointment, the other saw it as a personal slap in the face and mumbled that his partner wasn't shouldering his part of the load. When one partner was especially quiet, the other assumed it was an intentional snub and commented that maybe he wasn't good enough for the other.

Those two men fell prey to the power of little negatives. Their negative comments nurtured those little differences into a terminal illness for their friendship. They let little negative things black out all that was mutual and positive. If those two businessmen had only sat down and made a list of all the things they agreed upon when the business was founded, they would have been on the road to resolving the minor points of disagreement.

When negativism reigns, any disagreement becomes bad. That is why we need to work hard at seeing what is positive. Conflict can be the beginning of the solution to a painful and possibly long-standing problem. Is the other person's position all bad? We may tend to spend too much time analyzing what is wrong and spending little or no time analyzing what is right. It is surprising how much you and the other can agree upon. We should ask what the other person has done that is acceptable and build on that. We should do the same for ourselves.

The first positive thing is usually that we both desire a resolution. Obviously we do not desire the same resolution, otherwise there would be no dispute. But usually both people want an end to the conflict. Why not make that strong desire for a resolution the basis for a mutual process of seeking the solution? Working out the conflict will become the positive way to ending the pain of previously irreconcilable differences.

We will then be moving toward the positive goal of resolution and reconciliation. In the end we will be able to walk away from the conflict in the peace of allies, not as the victor and vanquished. Work on discovering many more points of agreement before you continue to build your list of disagreements.

Creating a Conflict Fantasy

Another thing that can make us think disputing is bad is to assume the worst. We need to be realists when assessing a dispute and only respond to what we know for certain is a fact. Avoid letting our worst fantasies run away with our emotions. For instance, do I know for sure that I can't talk to the other person? Is the other person really out to get me? Did he or she really say what was reported to me? Is the other person really going to do what I heard he or she might do? Are the other person's motives really what I think they are?

It all comes down to deciding that we will respond only to what we have seen and heard firsthand from the other person. All else is hearsay and possibly fantasy. Or worse, it may be our subtle way of creating excuses either to avoid solving the problem or to come out with both barrels blazing.

So, make sure to get all the facts and make sure your partner in the problem knows the facts as you know them. Share information, correct what is wrong, and discuss the facts face to face.

SUMMARY

Conflict can become a positive force if we develop a proper attitude toward it. Conflict is good when it leads to change and harmony. Learn to channel conflicts toward constructive good. Do not avoid them and hope they will go away. Since conflict can lead to good or bad, it is important that we develop skills that will bring out the good. The next chapters give more specific helps toward that end.

PART II

FIVE STEPS TO RESOLUTION AND RECONCILIATION

The very fact that you have lawsuits among you means you have been completely defeated already. Why not rather be wronged? Why not rather be cheated? (1 Corinthians 6:7).

CHAPTER 3
WHAT ARE WE AFTER WHEN WE ARGUE?

There are lots of ways to conduct disputes— some constructive, some not so constructive. The biblical way to dispute is to have both parties win. After all, the prize is peace, not personal vindication.

STYLES OF CONFLICT

What's your favorite style of disputing? We all have encountered various styles of disputing, ranging from aggressive to passive. Knowing about our own and others' personal styles of disputing will help us avoid either being the winner who takes all or being the passive victim who lets others' power cloud the issue.

If, for instance, you are more passive and I am more aggressive, our dispute may be settled on the basis of power rather than justice. You'll say to yourself, "Well, after all, he's the boss"; or "It's too scary to talk to her. She always gets mad"; or "No way am I going to bring this up to him. He's bigger than I am."

If we are aggressive, we will be tempted to use our power for self-serving ends rather than for resolving the problem. We may assert, "If you don't do what I'm asking, you won't get your allowance"; or "I'm your boss, and you have no choice"; or "It's *my* ball!"

Knowing about various styles of disputing can help diffuse our weak points and aid us in working together on common ground. We can recognize five different styles of conflict:

—I Win, You Lose
—Peace at Any Cost
—The Fifty-Fifty Style
—Away Without Leave
—I Win, You Win

I Win, You Lose

Meet the tough battlers. They are out to reach their own goals at all costs. They have little concern for others' needs, and they do not require acceptance—just winning. Losing brings reduced status, weakness, and loss of self-esteem. Winning brings exhilaration and status.

Do the tough battlers win? Always! They will support their convictions with enough anger and thoughtless comments to offend many. When others disagree with them, they go into their standard finale, "There's no use talking to a closed mind like yours!" End of conversation.

Since there must be a winner to every disagreement, there must also be a loser—you. Tough battlers are quite willing to sacrifice your dignity or worth if you do not go along with their position. For them, conflict is a nuisance that occurs only because others do not see the correctness of their own position. When they run out of facts, they are quite able to argue for their position by sheer bluster.

These people use many strengths, such as the ability to organize and express thoughts, but within a narrow and self-centered concept of winning. They think that winning defines their personality when it really only defines an issue. They center the debate on their own position rather than on what is just and equitable.

Peace at Any Cost

These people desire relationships over justice. They will let their own goals suffer just to keep their friends. Their need for acceptance by others pushes them into conformity with the desires of others, even when those desires are in conflict with their own. They are people who say, "Well, yes, there are some things I would like to have accomplished, but it's OK. I don't want to make trouble."

They feel that when differences are discussed frankly,

someone is going to get hurt in the process—most likely them. To them, conflict grows out of self-centeredness and should be avoided in favor of harmony. Anger is bad and confrontation is destructive. They try to redirect potential conflict by breaking the tension with humor or suggesting some less confrontational activity. Mutuality of interests and harmony of relationships are most important. What they end up with, however, are superficial relationships and the threat of hatred and resentment growing inside them. They grow to resent living with conflict brushed under the carpet.

These people have a key strength: they understand the ultimate importance of relationship. Uncontrolled differences only serve to drive people apart and the personal implications cannot be ignored. For most of us, to differ is to reject. Maximum attention, therefore, to the needs and desires of others is required if relationships are to endure. The peace-at-any-cost people, however, press for peace that sometimes compromises justice.

The Fifty-Fifty Style

The basis of this approach is that half a loaf is better than none. The fifty-fifty style doesn't address the personal issues of reconciliation, only the mechanics of a proper settlement. The fifty-fifty person enjoys the maneuvering required to resolve conflict and will actively seek to find some strong middle ground between two expreme positions. If I want to buy a car for $4,000 and my wife wants to buy new carpet, the fifty-fifty style will suggest a $2,000 car and $2,000 of new carpet. If Dad wants to go to the coast for a vacation and Mom wants to go to the mountains, the fifty-fifty style will suggest one week at the beach and one week at the mountains.

This approach's strength lies in its belief that differences should be treated in the light of the common good. Each party may be obliged to lay aside his own views in the interest of the majority. But it is never possible for everyone to be satisfied, and a simple dividing up of the disputed pie does not always do justice to the relative merits, priorities, and needs of the disputing parties. If Dad is going to complain for the week in the mountains and Mom is going to be grumpy for the beach week, perhaps a better solution would be to go nowhere or to look for another alternative that both parties liked.

Away Without Leave

The people using this style see conflict as a hopeless, useless, and punishing experience. Rather than undergo the tension and frustration of conflict, they simply remove themselves mentally or physically. Encounters with others are kept as impersonal as possible, and in case of disagreement, they'll withdraw. They'll agree to a resolution only in order to avoid disagreement and tension. They will feel little commitment to the decision reached, and they will not openly take sides in a disagreement among others.

These people need to learn that differences are not destructive. They simply reflect the more basic attributes that distinguish one person from another: past experiences, irrational needs, innate limitations, and levels of personal hopes. As such, they are essentially beyond the influence of others. For the away-without-leave people, however, conflicts are necessary evils in human affairs. These people drop their responsibility to seek justice and be peacemakers.

I Win, You Win

This approach acknowledges that resolving a conflict is not a power play; nor is it accepting a straight percentage of everyone's goals and forgetting the rest. It acknowledges that winning goes through the surface problem down to the interpersonal level. No one's goals need to be sacrificed if the appropriate resolution is achieved. The big surprise about this style is that you might get all the goods in a dispute and I might get nothing, but I could still find that my real goals were met. For example, I might refuse to pay a particular bill because I want to force you, the landlord, to give me a face-to-face hearing of my complaints. It is possible for you to end up with all you want, my rent, and yet for me to have my goal met, gaining a hearing and getting my complaints off my chest. Unlike the fifty-fifty style, equal satisfaction may be met without equal division of the spoils. This style works from several assumptions:

1) Conflict is natural and helpful; it can even lead to a more creative solution, if handled properly.
2) Feelings are legitimate expressions when working toward a resolution of conflict.
3) Everyone's attitudes and positions need to be aired. When conflict is resolved to the satisfaction of all, commitment to the solution is more certain.
4) Everyone involved should have an equal role in resolving the conflict; everyone's opinions are equally legitimate.
5) No one person should be sacrificed for the good of the group.

Differences are a natural part of our human condition;

differences themselves are neither good nor bad. Conflict is usually a symptom of tensions in our relationships and should be treated accordingly. When accurately interpreted, they may be resolved and may serve to strengthen rather than to divide our relationships.

Conflict requires confrontation and objective problem solving, often of a type that goes beyond the apparent needs and opinions of those of us involved. Not only are we brought more closely together when conflicts are worked through, but our creativity may also be developed.

Three Basic Approaches

The approaches to conflict discussed above come down to three basic styles.

First, we can go for a win. This resolution seldom leads to reconciliation. The outcome is victor and vanquished.

Second, we can give up and let the other side win. Here again, we seldom find reconciliation. The settlement is made, but we go away having to cope with our unresolved emotions and sense of injustice.

Third, we can decide that both sides will come away with a sense of justice and peace. In resolving the dispute, each of us gives enough to allow the other some win, and each of us keeps enough to allow the other to maintain a sense of fairness. That paves the way for reconciliation.

WHAT IS THE GOAL OF CONFLICT?

Winning and Losing

We are taught daily that life is a win-or-lose situation. Sports are won or lost. Court decisions are won or lost. Wars are won or lost. We win if we get the job, and we lose if we don't.

We tag our days, children, marriages, jobs, and even our lives as winners or losers. "She's a winner." "He's a loser." We are taught to "get out and win," which apparently necessitates that someone else will "get out and lose."

The truth is, we are losers only when someone tags us as losers. For example, are we really a loser just because we lost one race? What about the ten we won? Don't they count? What about the dispute we got into with our neighbor? Just because we disagree, does that make our whole friendship bad? Do we have to lose an entire friendship over one loss?

To many, losing is not just a disappointment; it is bad. Winning is not simply a pleasure; it is good. In other words, winning becomes a moral victory. With that moral veneer over winning and losing, it makes no sense to say, "Something good happened today. I lost." Because we do not want something bad, we avoid losing at all cost. We also wrap a false sense of goodness about ourselves each time we come away a winner. Winning does not make a person good. Losing does not make a person bad.

Take the morality out of winning and losing and put it where it belongs—in the fairness and justice of what was won or lost. If we are going to achieve reconciliation in a dispute, we are going to have to allow both parties to win something, regardless of how small.

Many times, when we are trying to resolve a dispute, we will say, "I have gone the second and the third miles, while the other party hasn't moved an inch." Then the other side will say about the same thing. Maybe neither side has moved far enough toward listening, understanding, and caring. If we truly get to the end of that first mile, we will have moved from self-defensiveness to sympathetic understanding—the bare minimum for resolving our differences.

Traveling along the second mile will teach us that even when we "lose," we can "win." We learn how to right a wrong. We learn how to turn the other cheek. We learn how to keep a good attitude while facing adversity.

Win the Person, Not the Argument

What are we after when we are drawn into a dispute? When we run up against an opposing viewpoint, do we feel the rush and drive to have our view prevail, even at the cost of some hurt for the other person? Do we go for the win and not think of the other person's need for dignity and respect? Do we think, "Well, if he's wrong, he's wrong, and that's all there is to it"?

The goal of conflict is resolution and restoration to an improved future. Jesus taught that goal in Matthew 18:15–19. He counseled, "If your brother sins against you, go and show him his fault, just between the two of you. If he listens to you, you have won your brother over" (Matt. 18:15).

Win the person, not the argument. Our goal is to solve our problems and keep our relationships intact.

Not all our disputes arise because someone sins against another. Our dispute may simply be the result of natural disagreement about something. Usually, however, those natural disagreements quickly turn into sinful actions.

Our goal, whether faced with disagreement or sin, is to put an end to the conflict by seeking to win the other person. We can win an argument but lose a friend. At heart is our desire to seek the right thing before God. That attitude leads to a principled approach to disputes that results in both sides experiencing justice and compassion. If our disputes end in personal splits, someone's goals were not right.

When faced with disagreements, our goal is to be a loving encourager. Between the two parables about the lost sheep (Matt. 18:10–14) and the unforgiving servant (Matt. 18:21–35), Jesus talks about restoring a fallen Christian, about winning the other person. Our goal in a dispute is to correct wrongs and win a purified relationship. That is miles apart from the goals of punishment, excommunication, or winning for our side.

THE LINKS OF RELATIONSHIP

How can both people win? The rest of this book will explain the links between our relationships and how we can put them back together again when they are broken.

First, we need to *examine ourselves* (chapter 4). Then we need to *appreciate God's forgiveness* (chapter 5). After that we need to *resolve our conflicts with the other person* (chapter 6). Finally, we need to *allow time for healing* (chapter 7).

For now, consider what prize you seek and what approach you take when faced with disagreements—from minor conversations to major catastrophes. The best prizes are peace, purity, and restored relationships.

Why do you look at the speck
of sawdust in your brother's eye
and pay no attention to the plank
in your own eye? (Matthew 7:3)

CHAPTER 4
RESOLVING OUR CONFLICTS
WITH GOD

*Before we march off to the other person
and start making things right, we may need
to clear up a few things. First, we have
to make sure we can stand before God
with a clean conscience.*

Our human nature leads us to believe that the first step toward resolving a conflict is showing the other person where he or she is wrong. We say to ourselves, "If only the other person would change, I'd have no problem."

That may be true, but how are *we* going to make the other person change? We can't; but we can change ourselves. If we truly want a dispute reconciled, we must start by examining ourselves. Because we are part of the problem, we can also be a powerful part of the solution.

We need to begin not by enumerating the other person's faults but by praying that God will reveal our own faults. We ask ourselves if we have offended God. We start with God and ourselves, not the other person.

ADMIT THAT WE ARE PART OF THE PROBLEM

One of the toughest hurdles in any dispute is to consider that we might be part of the problem. That may make us a bit uneasy, especially if the other person started the trouble. Can we take on some of the blame? Can we admit that we probably have some part in the problem—perhaps not in the start but at least in some points in its process.

Have we entertained some hurtful thoughts?
   —"Look at the sloppy way that person dresses."
   —"What a slob. I keep my house much more neatly than
      he does."
   —"The way she lets her kids run around really gripes
      me."
Have we spoken some punishing words of gossip?
   —"Did you hear about the mess the Hendricks got
      themselves into?"

—"Oh yes, Sarah has a history of saying dumb things."
Have we cloaked aggression in passive acts of rejection?
—"I'm not going to give them the time of day. When we
    pass, I'll just look too occupied to talk."
—"She's not going to get a warm and friendly hello from
    me."
—"If they knock on my door, I'm not going to be in."

Once the hurdle of recognizing our part in the problem is
jumped, we can start resolving the problem. That is the make-
or-break point of the rest of the reconciliation process. Until
we are willing to take our responsible place in our dispute
there is no point in going on.

Hidden Blindness

We must start the problem-solving process with ourselves. Though our reflex action may be to expose and correct
the other person's problem, Jesus desires us to begin by
looking at ourselves:

> Why do you look at the speck of sawdust in your brother's
> eye and pay no attention to the plank in your own eye? How can
> you say to your brother, "Let me take the speck out of your
> eye," when all the time there is a plank in your own eye? You
> hypocrite, first take the plank out of your own eye, and then you
> will see clearly to remove the speck from your brother's eye
> (Matt. 7:3–5).

It is always easier to see other people's problems. Though
Jesus certainly wants us to help clear up our fellow-believers'
problems, we need something more than the desire to right a
wrong. We need to be aware of our own problems.

Jesus used our eyes to illustrate that problem. When

there's something in them, we can't see properly. Jesus, however, was not concerned with ophthalmology; He was after a better way of seeing spiritually. He does not want us thinking we see clearly while He knows we are really partially blind. God does not want us to launch out to resolve our conflicts with other people while we have unexamined faults within ourselves. Clear up any conflicts with God and then go on to clear up conflicts with other people.

It is difficult to find the hidden blindspots in our own perspectives—we can't easily see them. But it is essential to clear up our outlook so that we "will see clearly to take the speck out of [our] brother's eye." Then we will be clear-sighted problem-solvers.

It is helpful for us to examine three common blindspots in our perspectives about conflict. First, *we punish others and excuse ourselves*. Next, *we retaliate with anger*. Finally, *we do not give our problems to God*.

BLINDSPOT #1: WE PUNISH OTHERS AND EXCUSE OURSELVES

Awareness of our blindspots and improvement of our clear-sightedness begins by answering an important question: Whose fault is it?

Do We Want to Make Them Pay?

What if we decide it is the fault of the other people? Do we ever want to punish the people who have hurt us? Do we want to make them pay? If so, our focus has gotten hung up on *them;* what *they* did and what *they* need to do in order to make things right. That focus goes all the way back to Adam and Eve, who blamed everyone else but themselves. Hurling blame, however, is actually only a game we play to keep from looking at ourselves.

When we make a mistake, we probably have many great excuses. What about when someone else fails? Isn't it all too easy to list the reasons why they are without excuse? To excuse our faults and condemn those of others is a common knee-jerk reaction. Our passionate investigation of who's to blame is usually more than an academic question. It can reveal a heart that wants blood, not just a simple answer.

Putting the Blame on Someone Else

"It's her fault; it's his fault." That response to conflict is all too common. When faced with a problem, we often look for someone or something else to blame. It was the neighbor's fault; my wife forgot to mail it; my parents would not let me; I had to do it or lose my job; he would have hurt me if I hadn't done it.

Most people in a confrontation start off by saying, "But look what they did to me"; or "Look what they said about me"; or "Can't you see it's all their fault?"

It is false to think that if we can just shove the blame off on the other person, then the matter is settled. We are off the hook, and now it is all up to the other person to set things straight. Because reconciling a relationship is more than an indictment, it must proceed far beyond blame. Let's look to ourselves first and leave the question of the other's faults until later.

Taking Responsibility for Our Errors

One of the hardest things for us to do is to admit that we are in the wrong. When a dispute arises, we must learn to ask what we have done wrong and how we can correct it. Even if the other person did wrong, that does not exclude us from starting the healing process by asking forgiveness for ourselves.

If we happen to be "innocent," we may not readily see what needs forgiveness. But when we look closer, we may begin to see anger and bitterness. Have selfish thoughts crossed our mind? Bitterness and hostility are just as wrong as committing the offense that began the dispute.

Start by considering our part in the problem. When we confess our own sin, we begin the process that will eventually remove any obstruction in our vision.

BLINDSPOT #2: WE RETALIATE WITH ANGER

The newspaper headlines read, "EX-EMPLOYEE KILLS HIS SUPERVISOR." Why did he do it? Was it for money or power? No, it was for anger.

For over ten years a grudge had festered within the man because, in his opinion, his boss had wrongly disciplined him. Early one morning his ten-year-old hidden rage became open vengeance. He waited by the entrance to his former boss's office and shot him when he arrived.

What a tragedy! If only the employee would have asked forgiveness from the Lord for his hatred and resolved his conflicts with his boss, many hearts would have been spared incredible pain. What a terrible set of scales his bitterness built. Only his boss's blood could balance out the weight of his anger.

Retaliation or Reconciliation?

It is impossible to predict the result of uncontrolled anger. If we allow anger to run its course in our lives, we may find ourselves facing lawyers, courts—even prison. In order to show what might happen to someone who let their anger fester rather than getting reconciled, Jesus cautioned that if someone put you in prison, you would "not get out until you have paid the last penny" (Matt. 5:26). The choice is simple. Either nip anger in the bud or open yourself up to far-reaching and severe consequences.

Anger and resentment creep in subtly. When a conflict arises, we may find it easy to come to God for help. We may also find that we have brought a lot of anger with us to the Lord. Our anger is not necessarily wrong, but we have to deal with it, not feed it. Then we will be able to look past the hurt and begin to see forgiveness.

Anger and Worship

The Gospels show that Jesus had strong feelings about the importance of dealing with our anger quickly and properly. He taught that our worship is unacceptable if we harbor any unreconciled relationships:

> But I tell you that anyone who is angry with his brother will be subject to judgment. . . . Therefore, if you are offering your gift at the altar and there remember that your brother has something against you, leave your gift there in front of the altar. First go and be reconciled to your brother; then come and offer your gift (Matt. 5:22–24).

Anger can block worship. Jesus told about a man who came to prayer with a heart full of worship. During that worship he remembered that his brother had something against him, something that had caused a breach in their relationship. In light of the bad feelings involved, he had a choice to make: continue on with his worship or heal a broken relationship.

Our own quiet devotion in church on Sunday or in the quietness of our room may be interrupted with a reminder of conflict. Will we choose to neglect the conflict and carry on with our worship, knowing we are angry with someone? If we do, we will open ourselves to some far-reaching consequences.

Anger: Starve It, Don't Feed It

The beast within. Anger is like a baby boa constrictor. When it is small, we can kill it under our heel. If we feed it, it grows. One day it will wrap itself around us and crush our emotional, spiritual, social, or physical life. Do not feed the beast! If we are angry, we need to ask forgiveness. Only then will we see clearly enough to work out our differences and live in peace with our neighbor.

A word from jail. The apostle Paul asks us to keep control of our anger: "If you are angry, don't sin by nursing your grudge. Don't let the sun go down with you still angry— get over it quickly; for when you are angry you give a mighty foothold to the devil" (Eph. 4:26–27 LB).

Paul was in jail when he wrote these words. He could have been bitter—after all, he had done no wrong. He could have had anger in his heart. Instead, he urged others to avoid anger. Unfortunately, we too often nurse our grudges, allowing our differences to distance us until the gulf is too wide to bridge.

Anger and the Cross. Any ill will that exists between us and someone else must end at the cross of Christ, not at the door of the other person. We are not strong enough to carry anger and a cross at the same time.

Jesus died on the cross for our sins because He loved us: "A new command I give you: Love one another. As I have loved you, so you must love one another. By this all men will know that you are my disciples, if you love one another" (John 13:34–35).

"As I have loved you. . . ." His death was a loving act on our behalf. That love should be mirrored in our love for others. We can be right without hating and proving the other person wrong. To resolve a dispute, we do not have to knock someone down mentally, verbally, or physically. If we lash out at someone, we first need to acknowledge our error before God and appreciate His forgiveness.

Let God Cleanse our Hearts

We need to examine our attitudes toward the one with whom we are in conflict. Do we feel bitter or resentful? Do we wish something bad would happen to that person? Are we trying to fool God and ourselves by thinking we can carry on with Him while all the time bringing our animosity with us when we pray? We may not be involved with lawyers and prison, but our harbored anger will have its own set of consequences. If we leave our feelings unchecked, we will pay those dues to the very last cent: dues of bitterness and quenching God's work in our lives.

We all know that we are unable to rid ourselves of these feelings. They don't go away. In fact, they often grow. We will live with our stubborn, negative feelings unless we confess them to God and ask Him to cleanse us. And His promises are reliable: "If we confess our sins, he is faithful and just and will forgive us our sins and purify us from all unrighteousness" (1 John 1:9).

BLINDSPOT #3: WE DO NOT GIVE OUR PROBLEMS TO GOD

The Struggle to Let Go

Even though we have confessed our errors to the Lord, we know that eventually we will have to ask forgiveness from the other person in the dispute. But what will happen then? How will we protect ourselves when the wheels of resolution get rolling? How do we know that it will turn out the best way?

Our feeling of panic will soon be overtaken by desires to scheme and manipulate. After all, who else but us will be looking out for our best interests? Those all-too-human thoughts require us to consider something else before we go to the other person. We must turn the entire process over to God.

Wait, first we have to be *willing* to turn over control to God. We must be willing to give up all manipulating maneuvers and let God handle it in His time and His way. The Bible counsels us to "Let him have all your worries and cares. For he is always thinking about you and watching everything that concerns you" (1 Peter 5:7 LB). God is for us, but the outcome may not be the one we would have chosen.

The Risks of Letting Go

The implications of letting go are far-reaching and very important for a final resolution of the problem. In fact, turning it over to the Lord is a big risk.

The risk of giving up control. To give it to the Lord means we give up control over the outcome. We open ourself up to the Lord solving the problem in a way we do not expect or perhaps even want. God might even change us.

God will resolve the problem, but are we willing to let Him do it His way? If we are, then our outlook will be clear for solving problems. We will move from being at odds with each other to being friends trying to work out the problem together. As Matthew 5:25 says, "Make friends quickly with your opponent at law while you are with him on the way. . ." (NASB).

The people on both sides of a conflict will have opinions about how the dispute should be settled, but if we have given the process and result over to the Lord, our attitudes will be different. We will see ourselves working out our differences together under God's guiding hand rather than slugging it out from our respective corners of a boxing ring.

Two Christian businessmen were in my office seeking help in resolving a dispute which had hurt their relationship and Christian example. Bill had loaned Robert a large sum of money on a short note. They had done that for each other in the past without any problems. This time, however, Robert did not pay it back in the time period they had agreed on.

Bill tried to collect but was unsuccessful. At that point he took it to his lawyer and filed suit. As the court date got closer, both men came to me and asked if I would try to mediate their dispute. After talking with them separately, I brought the two together in hopes of working things out.

After several sessions, I had gotten nowhere. I called the two men together, and we prayed about this matter. We asked God to take full control of the outcome. After prayer, I adjourned the session and started to leave, but Bill wanted to stay and talk.

He told me that he felt he was wrong by letting this matter go as far as it had and asked me to call Robert back so he could talk to him.

I ran down three flights of stairs and caught Robert just as he was ready to drive off. As we walked back into my office, I sensed a calm that had not been present before.

Immediately upon entering my office, Bill held out his hand to Robert and said, "I am sorry that I have let this matter come between us, and please forgive me for acting the way I have been acting. I am forgiving the entire loan; you owe nothing." With that he put his arms around his Christian brother and wept with joy. The burden of conflict had been lifted even though Bill had not caused the initial problem.

After a very short time Robert looked at Bill and said, "No, I am the one who is wrong. I need to ask your forgiveness, and I will repay you as soon as I get to the bank." As they both shook hands, they agreed to patch up the past and look to the future.

Until they turned it over to the Lord and allowed Him to work it out, they could not agree. Once the Lord was in control, the matter was resolved quickly, and the men were reconciled to one another.

The risk of faith. To give the outcome over to the Lord reveals the honesty of our faith in His ability. Do we have our mind made up about how the problem should be solved? So does our opponent. The presence of at least two conflicting ideas about the outcome is what makes a dispute in the first place.

The only way to get beyond that stalemate is openness to an outcome that might be different from the one we want. Can we believe that we are not trusting in a merely human outcome but in an outcome derived from the hand of a sovereign God? That may present us with a crisis of faith. Will we risk it? God is at work reconciling the world to Himself and can be trusted to work out our own need for justice.

The risk of openness. Total openness and honesty before the Lord is also risky. We cannot turn the problem over to the Lord without being truthful before Him. Openness before God will become the bridge to public honesty. Our openness will have to continue before people. Can we risk that type of public honesty? Only if we have first developed it in the forgiveness and love of God.

The risk of the future. Giving our problems to God involves a continual release of future problems and decisions to His control. We will be tempted to display pride, defensive maneuvers, an "attack" posture, manipulation, worry, or gossip to build ourselves up and to tear our opponent down.

It is one thing to give God control in the safety and solitude of our prayers. It is another thing to work that out in the stress and pressures of face-to-face problem solving. When things get tense, we should examine ourselves to see if we have forgotten Who is really in charge and Who is ultimately responsible and powerful to bring about a solution.

A CRISIS CHECKLIST

As we continue to think about our feelings and continue to trust God for solutions, we need to ask ourselves some important questions:

1. Where is the real problem? It is very important at this point not to be solution oriented, that is, focused only on how we can solve the specific problem. That time will come. For now we need to focus on the exact nature of the problem, especially the problem as seen from *both* sides. What do I want? What do they want? That will help us understand the basic problem.

2. What are our feelings in this conflict? Have we had

anger, harsh words or thoughts? Have we worsened the problem? Can we see our way clear to ask God to cleanse our hearts and enable us to forgive our neighbor?

3. What are we responsible for in this conflict? We are not placing blame at this point. We are seeking to perceive a full-orbed statement of all sides of the problem. This will put us on the track to discovering a solution to the argument because we have received the power to overcome our desires to hurt and to win at the other's expense.

4. Are we willing to go to the other person? We may not be ready, but are we willing to talk to the other person about the conflict? We may recognize that we still harbor too much anger or bitterness toward the person. This is where we see if we have been honest before God.

No one can clear up these blindspots for us. Only when we realize the depth of our own wrongness can we come to God and ask for forgiveness, cleansing, and direction. Then He will do His restorative work in us, clearing up our vision and allowing us to see the next step.

But he who has been forgiven little
loves little (Luke 7:47b).

CHAPTER 5
RESOLVING OUR CONFLICTS
WITH OURSELVES

This chapter takes us one step further toward settling our disputes. After we've located and confessed our errors before God, the next step is to consider how we feel about ourselves. Do we deeply appreciate our forgiveness? That appreciation forms the hinge between God's forgiveness of us and our forgiveness of others.

LEARN TO APPRECIATE OUR FORGIVENESS

Why is it so easy to bow our heads and ask God to forgive us? Why is it so hard to bow our pride and ask another person to forgive us? It is hard because we can move from God to people without fully appreciating our own forgiveness.

Before we can truly forgive another person, we must be full of the joy and conviction of our own forgiveness. In the heat of conflict, we are going to want to get angry and tell the other person off. How will we resist doing it? By sheer force of will? That works for very few.

The only way to avoid hating and hurting back is to be fully convinced of how good God has been to us. We are rotten like the other person—that is, we were going to hell, were we not? We are still capable of all the dirty tricks anyone else could come up with, are we not? The one difference between us and the world is that we are forgiven. Yes, we fail and rebel, but the blood of Christ cleanses us daily from all sin.

God does not condemn us. If that has really gotten through to us, we will be able to forgive and love people who are less than lovable. Jesus said that the one who loves much is the one who has been forgiven much (Luke 7:47). We will love only in proportion to our appreciation of how forgiven we are. If we do not have much to be forgiven for, we will not love much. The issue is not quantity of sin but quantity of appreciation of forgiveness. The Pharisee in Luke 7 did not see himself as needing much forgiveness. As a result, he had little love for Jesus. The woman, on the other hand, saw herself as needing much forgiveness. Her love for Jesus was great.

We are not better than the other person. In fact, if the person is a believer in Christ, we are equals. We are both sinners who have been saved equally by unmerited grace. So should we not forgive each other? The following story supplies a negative and positive answer to that question.

A DEAD-END FORGIVENESS

There once was a king who decided to call in all his loans: "As he began the settlement, a man who owed him ten thousand talents was brought to him" (Matt. 18:24). A debt of 10,000 talents was an impossible amount to repay. It amounts to several million dollars in today's money.

Because the slave could not pay, his master ordered him to be sold along with his wife, children, and possessions. Stunned, the slave threw himself before his master begging, "Be patient with me, and I will pay back everything." The master, pitying him, let him go and forgave him the debt (Matt. 18:25–27).

The slave had begged for an extension of time to repay the debt. He mistakenly believed he could eventually repay the enormous amount. The king knew, however, that cancellation, not repayment, was needed. Would the servant understand that the debt was forgiven, not extended?

> But when that servant went out, he found one of his fellow servants who owed him a hundred denarii [a few dollars]. He grabbed him and began to choke him. "Pay back what you owe me!" he demanded. His fellow servant fell to his knees and begged him, "Be patient with me, and I will pay you back." But he refused. Instead, he went off and had the man thrown into prison until he could pay the debt (Matt. 18:28–30).

The forgiven servant did not act forgiven. He missed the link between his own forgiveness and his forgiveness of others. He did not even recognize his own words before his master, now echoed back to him by his fellow servant.

Though he was very happy to be forgiven of his own debt, he had no desire to share that joy. He received extravagant forgiveness but offered none to others. At the heart of it, his *own ability to receive forgiveness* was tragically defective. He had no perception of the ongoing person-to-person implications of being forgiven. Forgiveness had found in that man a dead end.

The Consequence of Unforgiveness

Jesus told the story to illustrate the link between receiving and giving forgiveness. Peter had just asked, "Lord, how many times shall I forgive my brother when he sins against me? Up to seven times?" (Matt. 18:21). Peter's number seven hints at a small limit to forgiveness; the very smallness illustrated by the slave in the story. Jesus' "seventy times seven" expresses vast and unconditional forgiveness, the kind illustrated by the forgiving king.

The story does not have a happy ending. The slave's unforgiving heart was a massive affront to the grace of the king.

> When the other servants saw what had happened, they were greatly distressed and went and told their master everything that had happened. Then the master called the servant in. "You wicked servant," he said, "I canceled all that debt of yours because you begged me to. Shouldn't you have had mercy on your fellow servant just as I had on you?" In anger his master turned him over to the jailers to be tortured, until he should pay back all he owed (Matt. 18:31–34).

Since the slave would not mirror the king's forgiveness, the king would not forget the slave's debt and accordingly handed the slave over to the jailers.

Blocking or Passing Forgiveness?

That story is not just about a fictional slave and a king in a foreign land. It is about our willingness to mirror God's forgiveness in our own forgiveness of others. The link between God's forgiveness and our own ability to forgive is clear. The king felt compassion on him and forgave him the debt. The king told the slave he should have had mercy on his friend just as the king had had mercy on him.

Jesus ended the story with a warning, "This is how my heavenly Father will treat each of you unless you forgive your brother from your heart" (Matt. 18:35). Our debt to God is greater than the slave's to his king. Any wrongs that we sustain from others are as insignificant as the pennies owed by the fellow slave.

What wrong against us is so great that we have permission to act like the punishing and unforgiving slave? Unless we deeply comprehend God's forgiveness, how can we share with others what Jesus has done for us?

Our appreciation of forgiveness is the indispensable hinge between divine and human forgiveness. Before we are ready to pass forgiveness on to others, we must appreciate the mercy we have received from God.

If we make a mistake here, we may find that we have little or no desire to forgive anyone for anything. What forgiveness we might have will become worldly and sentimental, devoid of the power, love, and moral fiber of God's forgiveness in the Cross.

Jesus also taught that we are to forgive those who have wronged us—whether or not they have asked us to forgive them: "And when you stand praying, if you hold anything against anyone, forgive him, so that your Father in heaven may forgive you your sins" (Mark 11:25).

"Forgive them"—whether or not they have asked.

"Forgive them"—just you alone in the presence of God.

"Forgive them"—even before you go to them or they come to you.

In Christ's teachings we have the two sides of our personal conflict: our relationship to God and our relationship to the other person. Our need to forgive and to be reconciled with the other person is one with our need to be forgiven by God. Do we want God to forgive us? Then we must forgive others.

How Many Times Should We Forgive the Same Person?

Peter asked Jesus how many times he should forgive a person who had sinned against him. Thinking he was generous, Peter asked if it was adequate to forgive the other person seven times. Jesus responded by telling Peter that he should be prepared to forgive "seventy-seven times" (see Matt. 18:21–22). Jesus told Peter not to forgive once, but 490 times, if necessary. Jesus may have intended a symbolic number of infinite forgiveness, suggesting that we are never finished with forgiving others. We should keep no record of wrongs (1 Cor. 13:5) and forgive in love, with no strings attached.

Peter knew it was one thing to forgive different people, but he was concerned about how often he had to forgive the same person. We have similar questions when the person continues to offend us.

—"Am I not consenting to the other person's wrong-doing if I just keep forgiving?"

—"Isn't there an end?"

—"When is enough enough?"

—"Isn't there a time when for the good of everyone I should stop forgiving?"

Nearly every day we confront our need to forgive someone. Perhaps someone insults us. Or someone hurts our feelings. Someone promises to help us but doesn't follow through. We are put to the test daily. It is one thing to forgive many people one time each. It is quite another to forgive the same person many times.

We often have problems forgiving the second time, let alone the 490th. Forgiving a person the first time is often easier than forgiving the second or third time. Many times we draw a line and set our limit of one time and one time only. At that point, we have set a worldly limit and are failing to see the example set for us in Matthew 18:21–22. We must forgive without limits or conditions. We must also be serious in our forgiving. When we draw the line on forgiveness, hardness of the heart sets in. We must learn to forgive without limit or conditions.

The Joy of Forgiving and Being Forgiven

It feels great to forgive. If we have the hardness of an unforgiving heart, we will not like ourselves, and neither will our friends. When someone insults us or wrongs us, we can only look to God and forgive as He forgave. The bad feelings about ourselves for hating and hurting others will dissolve into peace and love.

The wonderful truth is that we can have that great feeling of forgiving someone without having to go to them. Eventually we will need to forgive them face-to-face, but we can begin by forgiving that person in our hearts, just between ourselves and God. If we are able to do this, we will be on our way to doing it with the person who has wronged us.

We are the keys to experiencing release from anger and resentment. Only we can ask forgiveness for ourselves. No one else can do it for us. Therefore we have no one but ourselves to blame for our bad feelings and guilt.

The importance of this cannot be overemphasized. Here is the moment when we, in the heat of a disagreement, will take the time to present ourselves before the almighty God for inspection. He will calm our emotions and release us from feelings of guilt and anger. To forgive another and ask for forgiveness from God is the foundation of resolution.

When we are confronted with problems and disputes that we cannot handle, the first step always should be to tell it to God. That is an obvious statement when we are cool. It is not so obvious when we are hot. Let Him know how we feel and why we feel that way. God always understands. When we tell Him our hurts and confess our hostilities, He will replace them with His love and understanding.

—"Dear Lord, I'm so mad!"

—*"Why?"*

—"Talking to Jim is like talking to a brick wall."

—*"What would you like to do to him?"*

—"I'd like to scream and punch him."

—*"That's your choice. But first let me tell you how I feel about him. I let my Son die for him. I love him. Now, what is your choice?"*

—"I'd still like to punch him."

—*"I know. By the way, I love you too. You're stuck. You can't get out of my love and forgiveness. I've made up my mind about that. That punch will hurt you more than it will hurt him. It will hurt me, too, to see you vent anger on one for whom my Son took so much pain. Would you forgive him?"*

—"For what?"

—*"For everything. I have."*

—"But he didn't hurt you."

—*"Yes, he did. By hurting you, my child. My Son paid the price for his sin against you. Why are you going to try to add to that price?"*

—"I'm so hurt, that's why."

—*"I know. My own hurt was infinite—for you and for him. Will you let the price Jesus paid for this particular sin suffice?"*

—"I'll try."

—*I love Jim—he was worth dying for. Is he worth your love?"*

—"Yes. But I've got to get our problem settled."

—*"I know. Forgive him right now, just between you and me. Love him the way I do, and you'll be ready for me to show you the way I solve conflicts."*

—"OK."

Put On Forgiveness

God offers to forgive our errors but that offer must be accepted for the forgiveness to take effect. Imagine yourself as a person who is in desperate need of clothing. It is raining, and you have no raincoat or waterproof shoes. Your shoes have holes and your shirt is torn. Then someone buys you new shoes, a raincoat, new jeans, and a wool shirt and offers the new outfit to you as a free gift.

You have several options. You can reject the gift, accept it and wear it, or accept it but leave it in the box and continue standing in the rain improperly dressed. Until you put the clothes on, you have not accepted the gift. Acceptance is not saying thank you; it is putting the clothes on.

It is the same with the gift of forgiveness. Until we put it on we have not accepted it. Until we have put on forgiveness for ourselves, we will not be able to walk through life forgiving others. Gauge our appreciation of forgiveness not by our warm feelings of gratitude but by our consistent acts of forgiving others.

WHAT IF I CAN'T FEEL FORGIVEN?

Sometimes we just might not feel forgiven. Yes, we know that God has told us in His Word that we are forgiven, but sometimes, especially in the more traumatic mistakes of life, we might have trouble putting our knowledge into experience. We lament: "I've just blown it too badly to be forgiven. How can I expect forgiveness for making the same mistake so many times?"

If we have trouble feeling forgiven, the real issue may be that we actually don't want to be forgiven. Not want to be forgiven? Sad but true. Here are some problems and solutions for not accepting forgiveness.

Are we forgiven in the first place? Maybe the reason we don't feel forgiven is that we really *aren't*. Perhaps we have not relied upon faith in God through Christ for salvation. Have we attended church for years but never come to grips with serious Christian beliefs?

Do we want attention or forgiveness? Accepting God's forgiveness means accepting human forgiveness—especially from the person we disagree with. That means the end to all the attention the bad situation has brought. No more telling of our woes and receiving great sympathy from our friends. No more making the other person grovel in order to get back into our good graces. Do we desire to get attention more than we desire to be forgiven?

For example, an offended wife may not want to receive her husband's apology because that would mean an end to all the special things her husband was doing to be accepted— sending flowers every day and calling her in the middle of the afternoon.

When her desire to punish ends, she will have to confess her errors and replace them with love. She might, however, decide it is better to keep the problem unsettled so that she can keep her husband on the line. She would rather keep the problem alive so that it can continue to be "corrected" rather than get on with a peaceful life.

Do we need encouragement? Perhaps we need help in prayer. Our pastor or a Christian friend could help in prayer and Bible study. Maybe we just need to spend some time with a friend who knows and supports us, who will affirm our worth. The encouragement of a friend or two cannot be overestimated.

Have we examined ourselves completely? If we cannot seem to feel forgiven, we can ask ourselves if we have missed something for which we need to be forgiven. We can go back to square one and search our hearts before God. God may be trying to help us make something right.

Do we really have anything to confess? Don't browbeat

yourself. God does not play hide-and-seek with our faults. Maybe the reason you can't seem to feel forgiven is a mistaken sense of guilt—in other words, thinking you need forgiveness when you actually have no sin to confess. Is it possible that you are under a false sense of guilt?

Do we feel loved? During a conflict we might have let our self-esteem drop very low. We may have forgotten how precious we are in God's sight. We will not be able to feel forgiven if we do not feel worth very much.

Danielle, who used to be a very trim 115 pounds, put on over thirty pounds during a time of conflict. David, who at one time dressed very well, could now care less how he looks. Those results of depression and low self-worth are common. When we forget that God loves us even when we sin, we will have trouble feeling forgiven.

Do we feel complete? Colossians 2:10 says, "In him [Christ] you have been made complete" (NASB), but many Christians do not realize that. We might use other ways of finding completeness: family, friends, success, church membership, activities in social events and community affairs. When we do not feel good about ourselves, we lie, brag, and exaggerate our accomplishments. We then feel guilty and we begin to lose our positive self-image. Feeling that way, we will not be able to feel forgiven.

Do we have peace? Christians who do not feel good about themselves often work themselves into ulcers, heart attacks, or nervous breakdowns. John 14:27 reminds us of Christ's promise: "I am leaving you with a gift—peace of mind and heart! And the peace I give isn't fragile like the peace the world gives. So don't be troubled or afraid" (LB).

SUMMARY

We need to see ourselves the way God sees us—in our sin and in our need for forgiveness. Seeing only our sin will lead to defeat. Not seeing our sin will lead to smugness. Seeing both sin and forgiveness will breed an honest and positive outlook. After all, we are totally forgiven and indwelt with the Spirit of God.

We then can think positively about ourselves and others. The only real basis others have for judging us is by our actions, and our actions are controlled by our thoughts. Once we turn our mind over to God, He can and will prepare us to feel forgiven and act out that feeling with others as we forgive them.

When a man's ways are pleasing
to the LORD, he makes even
his enemies live at peace with him
(Proverbs 16:7).

CHAPTER 6
RESOLVING OUR CONFLICTS
WITH THE OTHER PERSON

Now that we've examined ourselves and accepted God's forgiveness of our sins, it's time to go to the person with whom we have the conflict. It's time for a face-to-face reconciliation. This is where all our sincerity will be tested and where the Spirit will work a resolution of the problem.

A face-to-face talk with our opponents has great risk of hurting and great potential for healing. Because it can bring up all our worst fears and face-saving maneuvers, it is the time when all our private sincerity before God will be tested.

We may panic and want to run from the person. If we do meet, we may try skirting around the real issues with superficial talk. If we get down to the problem, we may take a hide or attack stance by either whitewashing our faults or condemning the other person's faults.

The best way, however, is to face the problem honestly, which is possible only when we are secure with God and ourselves. With our own life reconciled to God, we can reach out in reconciliation to others. Our first task is to work out a meeting with the other party.

ARRANGE THE FIRST MEETING

After many harsh words, fights, threats, and back-stabbing gossip, just getting two people to meet can be difficult.

— "The last I saw of him was the back of his head as he slammed my office door." Getting him back through that door will not be easy.

— "The last I heard from her was a loud *crack!* as she slammed down the telephone receiver." Getting her back on the line will be very tough.

When we try to get together with the other person, we must not be surprised if we are met with a cool or downright rude response. We must remember that our sincerity is being tested. We can expect several responses to our invitation to meet.

The put-down. When we indicate our willingness to

reconcile, we should not be surprised if we don't get a welcome and a thank you. It is a mistake to assume the other person has the same interest in resolution as we do. Each side in the conflict has many interests. Some will be the same, but many will be different. We must acknowledge the other's negative response as part of the problem and its solution. We must guard against letting the person's response hurl us into a defensive or hostile posture. How can we give full attention to the other person's best interests if we are worried only about our own? We might even be tempted to exclaim, "You idiot! Can't you see I'm trying to make peace?" Let's not trade one put-down for another.

No-show appointments. If we set up a time and the other person does not show up, be patient. Conflict breeds hostility, and we may just have received some of it. Our genuine love is being tested. Can we, as forgiven and loved by God, take a little of someone else's hostility in an effort to love and seek peace? Making us wait is a cheap shot, but just absorb the evil and move toward healing.

Always give the benefit of the doubt for having a reason for not showing up. Ask for another time. Avoid even a hint of blame such as, "Yes, let's plan to meet at the same place. It's amazing how many interesting things went on during the *hour* I waited for you."

The holier-than-thou response. "I'm glad to see you are finally trying to work out *your* problem." That type of response comes from people who have not yet admitted their own mistakes in the situation. The focus stays on the other people's problems so that they will not have to face their own. Will we respond to the pomposity or to the other person's worth before God?

The reserved attitude. The other person may not be ready to open up and be honest and forgiving. It took us time to come to that point. Give the other person space to come to the same point. We need to share where we are and make ourselves available to help.

Some people will wait a bit to see if we are really sincere. If we acted like an animal the last time they saw us, they may not be ready to believe the vision of saintly forgiveness that now stands before them. Can we blame them? Give them time.

Filling in the blanks. Silence. Unanswered notes. Unreturned calls. We probably tend to fill in silence with our worst fears or slanders. "I'll bet they are thinking and saying all kinds of bad things about me." Take silence for what it is: silence, neither good nor bad.

When possible, ask the person what he or she means by the silence, but only respond to a firsthand answer. Hearsay may convey only the third party's warped perspective, and we have enough problems already. Avoid coming to the discussion filled with anger and fears bred from filling in the blanks of silence with paranoia.

After reconciling our differences with God and ourselves, we are then ready to face all our problems openly with the other person. The release that comes from simply taking inventory of our lives and receiving the courage to do something about it is unexplainable. It is like a heavy load being lifted from our shoulders. And it is now easier to face the other person.

FOUR STEPS TO SETTING A POSITIVE TONE

Setting the tone is very important when we meet with the other person. An atmosphere of trust is vital. If we can come to feel comfortable and respectful toward each other, we will remove a major obstacle to peace.

On the other hand, if we start by putting each other down and showing no respect, we turn everything negative. A negative tone is highly contagious and can destroy the chance for settlement and reconciliation. The first words out of our mouths set the tone. Be positive, caring, and understanding.

1. Work Hard at Understanding Each Other

It is really a miracle that any information is communicated accurately. People hear things the way they want to hear them. Our version of another's words may be inadequate at best and at worst colored by our personal bias. Time and pressure also alter how we hear and repeat what we hear.

We say to our neighbor, "I told you I would do the repair work only if you bought the materials." We take for granted that our friend heard and understood the conditions of the deal. That may not have been the case. Commands and threats are often given without finding out if they are being understood. We will have to work very hard to assure that we both understand each other.

2. Realize that Hidden Tapes Are Playing

Often our goals and tactics in a dispute were given to us by our parents, pastor, or other people of importance in our lives. Our responses are often affected by messages that play in our heads like a tape recording. We may hear someone say to us, "Don't let them walk over you." Or maybe we hear, "Let them have it!" Or, "Stand up for your rights." These messages may not be relevant to the present situation at all, but they have become such an ingrained part of us that they trigger our own responses.

We may feel that the other person may also be responding to his or her hidden tapes. We need to consciously think of how we want to respond. Then we must pray that God will help us to respond positively and accurately.

3. Avoid Word Bombs

We must be careful not to use certain words or phrases: "I can agree with what you are saying, but . . ." A "yes . . . but" approach keeps replacing agreement with conflict.

Avoid put-downs like "don't be foolish" or "anyone can do that." They only keep fueling the fires of conflict.

Phrases like "believe me . . . " or "to tell the truth . . ." or "frankly . . ." imply that the previous words were less than true or frank.

We must try not to use words that express condescension or self-righteousness: "needless to say. . ." or "as you well know. . ." or "any fool knows. . . ."

We can help create a trusting atmosphere by using comments that show respect, sincerity, positive emotion, statements of agreement and openness.

4. Be a Good Listener

We must learn to become active, attentive listeners. We must respond when appropriate, not just sit in silence. Our faces can be responsive while we maintain eye contact. Phrases like "I see" and "yes" show sincere interest.

If we paraphrase what the other person is saying, we will know for sure that what we are hearing is what the other person is saying. We can ask, "Are you saying that . . . ?" or "Is this what you mean?" Not only will we better understand what the other person is saying, but we also will show that we care about the other person's opinions and thoughts.

People listen better if they feel that we have understood them. They tend to think that those who understand them are intelligent and sympathetic people whose own opinions and ideas are worth listening to. If we want the other side to listen to and appreciate us, we must begin by demonstrating that we are willing to listen to them. In addition to showing that we have understood, it helps to acknowledge that their ideas are needed to solve the problem.

FIVE KEYS TO RESOLVING A PROBLEM

Once we have faced the challenge of getting us together and have considered how to set the proper tone, we are ready to get down to the business of working out a resolution. Five basic steps guide the way:

1) Agree on the objective facts.
2) Communicate clearly.
3) Understand the personal dimensions.
4) Find some acceptable solutions.
5) Make the agreement.

1. Agree on the Objective Facts

Once we get together, we must give immediate opportunity to get all the facts of the case out into the open. Now comes the time when we begin speaking to each other—something that may not have happened for a while. The task at hand is to make all our knowledge mutual. We tell our side and listen to the other's. On our side, remember: no hurling of blame—just a recounting of the objective facts of the situation. We can follow this basic checklist:

Get the details of the case. Each of us should now tell our side of the story. This will involve us in dialogue as we add to and correct each other's input. The goal of this exchange is twofold: 1) to get the full picture of the case before both of us; and 2) to gain a basic unity about the factual areas of our dispute.

What is the sequence of events? When trying to expose the details, make sure we both have the same view of sequence. Understanding when things happened prepares for an enlightened discussion of causes and effects. For example, try to sort out the sequence of events, especially when the problem began. It is necessary for both sides to work through this problem to know who, what, when, where, and why it began. We can do this jointly or separately and then compare our notes.

Who said and did what? Remember, stick with the facts. Don't presume to know *why* things were said or done. Arguing about motives is a sure way to keep a conflict hot. Make sure both sides agree about who was behind what was said and done.

What are our assumptions? We must make sure that we do not mistake our assumptions about the issue for the facts. Our assumptions are the ideas and judgments we take for granted, even though we have not proved them to be true. We must move beyond our assumptions—which can be false—to the facts: information that can be proved to be true.

Before we make our final judgments, we must look at the facts and our assumptions about them. Fact one: The woman next door drives into your car. Fact two: She doesn't tell you about it. What are your assumptions? She is trying to swindle you out of a settlement. She is deceptive and wants you to think someone else did it.

As a result of your assumptions, you demand that she pay

for the damage right away. But as you probe deeper into the conflict, you discover that the reason she didn't come to tell you about it earlier was because she has no insurance and can barely feed her family as it is. Once you are aware of this fact, you revise your demands. You work out a repayment schedule that allows her to pay you in small amounts over a long period of time. More complete facts may not change responsibility for a problem, but they can change the fairness and form of the solution.

2. Communicate Clearly

Several principles will help us become more effective communicators:

Ask leading questions. Seek to probe to the heart of the situation. Ask leading questions that will encourage further discussion of the subject. Move from asking general to specific questions. Try always to encourage the other person to be more specific. When someone says, "You never listen to me," we can ask, "Can you be more specific?" The other person may then tell us that he or she is offended because we never stopped doing whatever we were doing when they talked to us.

Keep on target. Try to keep the discussion on the topic by systematically pursuing an issue long enough to deal with it thoroughly. Make sure both sides know where the other person stands before moving to another issue. For example, "Let me interrupt. We've covered three of the four points we needed to. Could we discuss the fourth point and summarize our positions before going on to something else?"

Be aware of changes in the emotional climate. We must be sensitive to changes in our emotions as we communicate. Is the other person starting to fly off the handle after being fairly calm? If so, try to keep emotions on a calmer level; try to decrease the emotional content of your conversation. For example: if you're discussing the other person's actions, do so without labeling those actions as either good or bad. Just describe the actions, like this: "Each time I propose an alternate solution for one issue, you begin talking about another issue without reacting to my proposal." Or, if emotions are getting out of hand: "Let's think this over for awhile, cool off, and then continue."

Keep the climate cool by not making accusations or generalizations about motives, attitudes, or personality traits. Lower the frustration level by staying on the subject; avoid constant shifts from one problem to another. Don't dodge issues—that just creates the appearance of being secretive and slippery. But do reduce tensions by knowing when to move on to another area if things are getting deadlocked. You can always return when the emotions get more under control.

Listen with empathy. We must be ready for a surprise when we share points of view. If we listen in love, we will find things look quite a bit different when we stand in each other's shoes. Standing in the other person's shoes—even for a few minutes—often results in deeper understanding and tolerance. This may be the first time we have sat down and really listened to each other's side of the story.

3. Understand the Personal Dimensions

The dispute started over some disagreement. You wanted **X**; the other person wanted **Y**. That is the objective problem. Then another problem arose—a personal one. Different from the objective problem, this one breeds in the shadows of anger and fear.

Neil was a hard worker for God. He taught a Sunday school class, was at all church functions, and was convinced that most of his salary should be spent on helping those in need. The family car was in constant disrepair, and the house needed fixing. Neil had little energy left for his family.

Neil's wife, Elaine, was fed up with the strain of trying to run a house on practically nothing and run her life with almost no care and understanding from her husband. Neil couldn't understand Elaine. Wasn't he working hard for the kingdom? Why couldn't his wife understand how much good he was doing?

Neil failed to separate the objective problem from the personal issue. Elaine was not against the work of God's kingdom; she just had some unmet personal needs. Neil seemed oblivious to her deeper needs for a husband. With each argument between Neil and Elaine, tensions and misunderstanding continued to escalate.

And so it can go for anyone who is not sensitive to the underlying personality problems in a conflict. Unkind words sparked anger. Hostilities escalated. No longer is the issue a new fence or a softer volume on the stereo. Because of the abusive words, the quality of our character, our worth as a person, and perhaps even our mother's reputation are being attacked. Now, even if the objective problem could be settled, a deep and open personal wound remains. That wound needs as much attention as the objective problem.

We must learn to separate the personal issues from the objective issues. Is it money or an apology that is really desired? John entered negotiation with his neighbor because of continued irritation with his neighbor's dog barking at all hours. John wanted a cash settlement of $500 to compensate for the nuisance. In examining the issues, it was clear that John did not value the money as much as he valued the neighbor's apology. The money was only a vehicle to get his neighbor's attention. The important issue was John's desire for an apology and respect.

When we probe into the reasons for a conflict, we often discover that the other person only wanted recognition or understanding. Take Eleanor, for example. She was a hard-working, dedicated employee who had worked for her employer for seventeen years. She would work late and come early just to get her work finished. Other employees would do only enough to get by. Eleanor felt she was being taken advantage of. She was doing more work than the other employees, and her boss knew it. Yet he just expected more.

One day, after letting this matter cause her many sleepless nights, Eleanor quit. She was convinced that she was no longer appreciated. Though she wished she had not quit, she was too proud to ask for her job back.

Shortly after getting Eleanor and her boss together, the problem was resolved. Her boss expressed his deep appreciation for all of Eleanor's work in the past—something he had never voiced before. He agreed to review her work load. They both were happy with the results, and both learned not to take a person for granted. They found a solution that met both of their needs. When Eleanor's boss recognized and appreciated her work, she was happy to return to the job.

4. *Find Some Acceptable Solutions*

Now that we have examined the facts, communicated our ideas clearly, and considered the personal dimensions of the conflict, we are ready to discuss solutions to our problem. We may find it hard to get beyond our own pet ideas, but if we have worked hard on seeing the other's point of view, we will succeed.

It is important to remember that a solution can be reached in a variety of ways. We must stay open to the other person's suggestions. We need to remain flexible, even retracing the various steps of resolution, if necessary.

If we want the other people to listen and understand our reasoning, we must avoid forcing our conclusions on them right away. If we begin by giving ultimatims, we will only alienate them.

A sure way to block a resolution is to make our demands so tough that the other person could never live up to them. It's easy to come to the settlement and say, "Here are all the requirements you will have to meet." That can put the skids on a settlement. We will have to work through the steps of the resolution with the other person, making sure we are willing to listen to the other person's ideas for resolution. We can come back with a counter proposal like, "I have taken what I think are the top four priorities for the settlement; are they correct?"

Trade-offs for peace. A dispute can be resolved in one of two ways: either the solution favors only one side or the solution pleases both sides. Finding solutions that satisfy both sides is a process of give-and-take. If we both are reconciled to God and to ourselves, we *can* be reconciled to each other, even if it isn't easy. That often means each of us may have to give up something.

In the majority of disputes, one side or the other has to give up something: we may give up a night with friends in order to spend a night with our spouse; we may give up a shopping trip to stay home and do repairs that need attention; our children may need to learn to give up playing with friends in order to finish homework or do chores. Whatever the case may be, someone usually has to give up something.

We need to avoid getting bogged down in the small details of the resolution. The good or bad points of any one part of the problem should not determine whether the solution as a whole is acceptable. Both of us should be willing to endure some pain to reach an acceptable settlement. We may abandon or compromise positions that we at first had claimed were not negotiable.

One young couple moved back from the brink of divorce and asked each other for forgiveness. They were willing to make changes in their lives, and they now had to live them out. Tom is a workaholic and would work late many evenings. Margaret is a perfectionist. She would have dinner ready at 6:00 each evening, but Tom wouldn't show up. He would decide to work late, but he would never bother to call her.

When Tom finally came home, dinner would be cold and Margaret would be hot. He could not understand what she was so angry about, and she could not figure out how he could be so insensitive.

Tom was the type of person who would get involved with whatever he was doing and forget that he was to be home at a given time or meet someone. Margaret, on the other hand, was just the opposite. If she was to be somewhere, she would be there on time, not late. If dinner was to be at 6:00, that is when it would be, not earlier, not later.

When they filed for divorce, this was only one of the many things that had to be worked out. Tom had to change, and Margaret had to learn to be more tolerant of his ways.

This was not the cause for the divorce, it was only one of many little things that had built up until the mountain got too high to climb over.

Once they started talking that problem out, they were able to laugh about it. Tom now calls if he is going to be late, and Margaret works even harder to make sure dinner is a relaxing time for the whole family. If he is late and forgets to call, he has agreed to bring her flowers. She seldom gets "late-for-dinner" flowers.

In the case of a parent who has a rebellious child, both have to give up something in order to be able to live together. The parent has to listen to the child, and the child has to respect the parent. The parent has to be open-minded, and the child has to be tolerant of the parents. Gaining the prize of peace is not equal with getting our own way.

Count the cost of settlement without reconciliation. The secular system for settling disputes is through the courts. Resolution takes the form of a settlement, but it stops there; it rarely goes beyond settlement to the essential stage of reconciliation. The objective problem may be settled, but the personal problems often go unaddressed and unhealed.

John had borrowed a large sum of money from Marvin. A disagreement arose about how much interest was being charged, and John stopped paying on the loan. After a short time, Marvin took John to court. The court dug out the ugly skeletons of each of the parties, dragged in close friends to testify, and sent out investigators to uncover whatever they could find about each of the men. The financial cost of all that was nothing compared to the indignity suffered by both sides. The court made its decision, and Marvin won a settlement. Though John had to pay according to the court-imposed settlement, the hard feelings persisted.

Although the courts solved the external problem, it did not set the stage for reconciliation. After two years of not talking to each other, John and Marvin asked to have their differences mediated. After several meetings, their differences were reconciled, and they are able to be friends again.

When we are tempted to continue with our feuds—perhaps even into court—we need to consider if we can afford the cost of getting our pound of flesh without healing the wound.

Move toward agreement. As we begin to approach a workable agreement, there are three principles that must be kept in mind: *translate and summarize* the major points of agreement or disagreement; *be flexible;* and *avoid ultimatums.*

Translate and summarize. Be able to translate and summarize points of agreement and disagreement. Translate the issues into relevant questions that focus on main positions or opinions. For example, "Is it your position, then, that you should receive the same consideration and respect now as you received before your marriage?"

Be flexible. It's all too easy to get locked into our first heat-of-the-moment, black-and-white demands. "It's this way or no way!" But both sides need to see that there may actually be several acceptable solutions to the problem. We are looking for a way for both of us to win and to reconcile our differences, and if we're to accomplish that goal, all possibilities for resolution must be explored. That involves discussing not only our demands and responses but also realistic alternatives. Too often we quickly agree to disagree without any real effort to explore possible trade-offs from which a settlement could be reached. Without that type of flexibility in our negotiations, we're likely to paint ourselves into a corner.

Avoid ultimatums. Before you drop a bomb like, "And this is my final offer!" consider what can happen if your bluff is called and your demand is turned down. Resolution ceases. Can you afford that? The one who offers an ultimatum has ceased to talk and work towards a solution. He has pushed the negotiations to the edge. The next step is to walk away— either as the total victor, or as the confirmed enemy. When your untimatum is turned down, then you'll have to quickly find some alternatives or negotiation will abruptly end.

5. Make the Agreement

Forgive and forget. Too often, our response to the need for forgiveness is, "Okay, I'll forgive—but don't expect me to forget it." Interesting. The sin is forgiven but not forgotten. What is the result of remembered sin? Well, first of all, it is impossible to forget a sin. It goes into our memory banks. Even when God says He will forget a sin, it does not mean that it goes out of His memory.

The writer to the Hebrews says, "And I will be merciful to them in their wrongdoings, and I will remember their sins no more. God speaks of these new promises of this new agreement, as taking the place of the old one; for the old one is out of date now and has been put aside forever" (Heb. 8:12–13).

And in the Old Testament Jeremiah says, " 'No longer will a man teach his neighbor, or a man his brother, saying, "Know the LORD," because they will all know me, from the least of them to the greatest,' declares the LORD. 'For I will forgive their wickedness and will remember their sins no more.' " (Jer. 31:34).

What does it mean to forget a sin? It means that the sin is

no longer a factor in how God will treat someone. It should be the same with us. We may remember the wrong someone did to us, but we will no longer take it into account in our relationship to that person. That is the basis for not only making an agreement but also living up to it.

A simple approach to closing the agreement. We can agree with someone and still not make an agreement. We can say the right words, "Yes, I agree that that is the best way for us to resolve the problem," or "Well, give me some time to think about it." But until we follow through on our words, we have not really agreed.

An agreement is the point where we put our terms of resolution into action. Some agreements will involve only some words and a handshake. Other situations will require a written agreement.

A basic approach to making the agreement is to review either verbally or in written form what has taken place and what will happen in the future. An easily remembered format is to outline the following:

1. What will have to be added to our lives to carry out the resolution?

2. What will have to be subtracted from our lives to keep peace and to keep the problem from recurring?

3. How will we specifically carry out those additions and subtractions?

4. When will we carry them out?

Those four points can be remembered as:

—**Plus** (What needs to be added?)

—**Minus** (What will be subtracted?)

—**How?** (How will it be done?)

—**When?** (When will it be done?)

If we find that a written agreement is necessary, we may want to use the formal agreement form found in the Appendix. Make sure both sides understand all of the facts about the disagreement; make no assumptions. Then outline the agreement in very specific terms.

CONCLUSION

Always look forward, not back. Our needs will be satisfied if we talk about where we would like to go rather than where we have been. Instead of arguing about the past, talk about what we want for the future. Instead of justifying what was done yesterday, ask each other what needs to be done tomorrow. When we talk about where we are going, we are setting goals. When we look back, we are worrying about things that cannot be changed.

Never be premature in final decisions of how to resolve the dispute. We will make wiser decisions if we first look at all possible answers. Wise decision making comes from a process in which we select from a large number of possible answers, not just our favorite one. Be loving and forgiving of others so that we too may obtain mercy and forgiveness.

Forgetting what is behind and
straining toward what is ahead, I
press on toward the goal to win the
prize for which God has called me
heavenward in Christ Jesus
(Philippians 3:13b 14).

CHAPTER 7
ALLOWING TIME FOR HEALING

*Resolving our outward problem is only the
threshold to personal reconciliation.
People have long memories, and those
memories can either help or hurt the healing
process. The past can be a wicked tormentor
or a wise teacher. This chapter shows how
to draw up a personalized agenda that
prepares us to cope with the long-range
consequences of our dispute without bowing
to others' punishing tactics or hardening
ourselves to the beauties of healing.*

BEYOND RESOLUTION

The dispute is settled. Now comes the time for planning the future and letting God heal the past. That is a real challenge. To think our work is done would be a great mistake. Our work on the person-to-person level will enter a new and crucial phase.

All the effects of the conflict will not be instantly erased. All the causes of hard feelings will not disappear overnight. Our initial problem can be resolved, but the conflict's consequences remain. The healing process demands extensive patience and love. We made it through the crisis, but can we keep it up through the aftermath?

Resolved and Reconciled?

Though our initial conflict may be resolved, what about the deeper more personal level? How do we feel toward the other person? How are we responding to the way the dispute was settled? Are we getting along with the other person? Is our friendship renewed?

We may say to ourselves after we have resolved the problem, "Our problem was solved. Why is there still tension between us?" The reason why tension and hard feelings can continue is because there is a big difference between resolution and reconciliation. Resolution is distinct from reconciliation in this way: *resolution is problem centered; reconciliation is healing centered.*

Problems are resolved. People are reconciled. It is possible to resolve differences without being reconciled. God resolved the conflict of sin by the death of His Son. He is willing to be reconciled to the world, but the process is not complete until the world is reconciled to Him:

Therefore, if anyone is in Christ, he is a new creation; the old has gone, the new has come! All this is from God, who reconciled us to himself through Christ and gave us the ministry of reconciliation: that God was reconciling the world to himself in Christ, not counting men's sins against them. . . . We implore you on Christ's behalf: Be reconciled to God (2 Cor. 5:17–20).

When a dispute is resolved, we walk away from a conflict that is past history. We also, however, walk *to* something: the world of the present. There we will find issues still in need of resolution and reconciliation. How will we face those who know about the original conflict? How will we handle our memories?

WHAT TO DO WITH MINDS THAT NEVER FORGET

"Oh yes, I remember him. Wasn't he the one who was arrested two years ago for shoplifting?" Kevin had been charged with stealing minor items from a local store. He was a prosperous businessman, and everyone in town knew him. Not only was he arrested and charged, but the newspapers ran the story—a devastation to Kevin and his family.

He made restitution and was ordered to do community service. That was bearable. The real agony came from his co-workers and friends. His prominent position in the community was shattered. He now had to start all over building trust and moving forward, not looking back. The healing process in this case will take years, not only for Kevin, but for his entire family. When he met his friends after his problem had been resolved, he still had to have answers. He also, in many cases, had to be the one to start the conversation.

When returning to the community after a dispute, we

must know what we are going to say and how we are going to greet those who did not approve of our past behavior. People have long memories. That can be a blessing or a curse. Either way, it is a fact of life in the healing process.

Forgive and Forget

Forgive and forget. When we are in the process of healing, those can be the most beautiful or the most cruel words we have ever heard.

They are beautiful when they signal the kind of forgetting that allows us to return to the place we had in the community before the conflict. Oh yes, everyone will remember from time to time that black page in our lives, but they will not treat us according to it. Instead, they will treat us as they did before it happened. That kind of true forgetting and true reconciliation goes beyond forgiveness and demands time. True forgetting is our restored state in the community.

Forgive and forget you. "Forgive and forget" also has its dark side. At its worst it means, "I forgive you, and now I intend to forget you." That is not usually said in so many words. It is simply the consequence of a piously covered series of so-called restorative moves. The errant parties are forgiven and then shunned.

Post-forgiveness banishment. A youth pastor who had gotten into tax trouble finally settled his fiscal problems. His church told him he was forgiven and restored. Afterward, however, he was excluded from his customary functions during public services. No reason was given for this, but the reason was clear. Words of forgiveness and restoration floated easily out of people's mouths, but actions that validated those words were blocked by stubborn hearts.

A forty-nine-year-old woman had been estranged from her daughter for twenty years. She said her daughter would never forgive her. Even after the problem had been resolved and the woman reunited with her daughter, she still wondered how her daughter could really forgive and forget. The pain of the problem was still strong in her mind. They were together but still apart on the inside.

An assistant pastor was caught in immorality, but he repented. The church publicly forgave him but dismissed him from the pastoral staff without any counseling from the pastor or the staff. The man turned to professional counselors for help, and after one year of psychological care, the therapists felt that he had made a full recovery. But the church refused to re-ordain him.

Restoration? No. The man was told that because of a few people who were unwilling to accept him back as minister, he would have to seek employment elsewhere. He was allowed to remain at his church as a layperson. He eventually found a job at another church—not an act of his own church's restoration.

What did forgiveness mean in this case? It meant, "We love you and forgive you and believe God wants you back in the ministry—but not here."

What was beyond forgiveness? Certainly not restoration. He was neither restored nor reconciled at his church because the leadership of the church allowed some people to keep punishing that man for his sin.

This post-forgiveness banishment is like a man who was fired from his insurance job but then was given a decent reference by his former boss. The boss said, "You are qualified to sell insurance—but not with this company." Is that employee restored by being sent off to another state? If someone said to you, "I forgive you, but you can never have the love and respect I gave you before," how would you feel? Forgiven? Reconciled? No. You would feel like a loser; someone who had made an irreparable error.

Pressing for Forgiveness

When we are faced with responses similar to those above, we must remember this. If we are right with the Lord and have done all we can to bring about resolution and reconciliation, we bear no guilt. Any ongoing punishment that others try to justify is bred from some sin in their own hearts.

We are forever obligated to press toward forgiveness and seek reconciliation to the last person. That may never happen on this earth. Just as God will never cease to reconcile the world to Himself through the gospel, so we must never cease trying to complete our smaller circle of reconciliation.

Discerning hollow forgiveness. When facing possible cold shoulders and exclusion by our friends, we must remember that sin is either forgiven or it is not. There is no half-forgiving, half-accepting, or half-reconciling. God's forgiveness was accomplished at the Cross, nearly two thousand years ago. When we believed in Christ, our own personal forgiveness and reconciliation with God was instant.

With other people, however, the process of forgiveness and reconciliation starts and stops according to individual weaknesses. Ideally, forgiveness would be instant. Reconciliation would soon follow, unencumbered by latent hardness of heart. Understand, however, that when we are faced with unforgiving hearts or legalistic conditions for reconciliation, we are being faced with sinful behavior, no matter how well intentioned or piously covered. Words of forgiveness followed by coldness betray their emptiness. Words of reconciliation followed by exclusion mock the foundation of God's work at the Cross.

That does not mean that we can mount an attack upon our errant friends. It just means that we need to see things for what they are and to move ahead in reconciliation with a clear conscience before God.

Knowing when we're forgiven. We will know we are forgiven when:

— People continue their relationship with us at pre-conflict levels.

— People show acts of love and encouragement.

— People are receptive to us in word and greeting.

— People are warm, not cold.

— People are human, not procedural, curt, or perfunctory.

— People look at us and are not distant.

— People stop gossiping about us.

The signs of forgiveness are unmistakable. Be lavish in your own display of them to all those involved in the healing process. Give warm thanks to those who display them to you.

The Time of Conditions Will End

We need to realize that the time of healing will demand certain conditions from us. For example, if we were forgiven for poisoning the neighbor's bark-all-night dog and then turned around and poisoned his next dog for the same offense, our chances of moving on in the healing process would be severely hampered. One absolute in the healing process is that the original offense not be purposely repeated.

To enjoy reconciliation, we will have to decide how to

keep the problem from happening again. That may take a referral to doctors, psychologists, or pastors. Each healing process is different. If we feel someone is demanding too much of us, consider this. Perhaps it is a condition for which we need to put ourselves out in order to go the extra mile, especially if we are the one trying to reestablish our credibility.

HOW TO FACE PEOPLE AGAIN

Even though Harold had settled his dispute with his employer and had reconciled his problems with his supervisor, he found that everything was not as it was before the dispute. Some employees avoided him; some were all smiles.

The more open the dispute, the more apt people are to take sides. Harold found he had to rebuild trust not only with his supervisor but also with the other employees and with the management. Some people accepted Harold completely, but some waited for him to slip up again. Other people had merely written him off.

Harold found he had to prove himself all over again and work harder to regain his worth and trust. We will encounter the same thing as we heal from our disputes. Our task is to take each person and, one by one, heal each broken link in our relationship.

We just worked out a resolution of our problem, and now we raise our heads to find an even larger group of people who, in one way or another, have a wound for which they hold us responsible. Where did all these unreconciled people come from? Though they probably had nothing to do with the original dispute, due to our direct or indirect actions in the dispute, these people have taken it upon themselves to have a dispute with us. They are offended. They are saddened and hurt. They are angry.

Those responses can be legitimate or they can be a product of our human nature that feels obligated to get stirred into someone else's business. Facing the various people whom we have indirectly offended is a very scary and defeating experience, but do not lose heart. With God and a few friends, we will have more than enough ability to heal the crowd, wound by wound.

Making the Rounds of Healing

The most important part of the healing process is talking with each person who is not reconciled to us. No amount of notes, calls, or interceding friends can do as much as one face-to-face talk between us and the other. We will have to prepare for each meeting. The problem neither happened nor will go away overnight. We and others will have to go back and develop our whole relationship and trust over again.

Know what to say. We have to anticipate what we are going to say. Think of each person and prayerfully discern the nature of your mutual problem. What is it that they hold against us? Do we have any idea of what they expect or desire of us at this point? What could we say that would be appropriate? If we see the need to ask forgiveness, ask yourself (or them) how we have wronged them.

Take abuse. Anticipate how we will respond to negative reactions. It all comes down to our ability to follow Christ's way of regaining unity in His Spirit by taking abuse without blasting back.

Work out a plan. If appropriate, work out some specific plans between the two of you to encourage reconciliation.

Think in both long-range and short-range activities. Coffee tomorrow? Dinner with the families next month? Cut firewood together next weekend?

Be sensitive. Test the emotional waters. Some people will let us move right back into relationship. Others will want us to be more reserved and slowly build the trust factor back again. A note we send may not receive a quick answer. Perhaps our warmth will meet only a cool reception. Let our emotions be appropriate to meet the other person's needs for healing so the relationship isn't divided further.

Be the better person you are becoming. We must realize that our task is not to become someone made according to the designs of those who have something against us. We are there to reconcile, not to re-create our personalities. We do not change everything because of one failure. Just change enough to correct the problem.

Because the healing process can surround us with so much negativism, we will have to work to keep a correct focus on the proportions of good and bad. Neither you nor the situation is all bad. We are simply remodeling one room, not building an entirely new house. God allowed that minor or major upset to refine us and make us a better person. Stay true to that better person in spite of the negative pull of criticism.

Open up to God's future. Be prepared for things to be different. When we are in the early stages of conflict, we may not be able to think about our future, but as the process moves on, we need to develop a plan for the future. How will our lives be affected by the people whom we have offended?

We will be challenged more than once to manipulate the healing process to further what we think are our best social interests. That uses and dehumanizes the person for our ends.

Resist. Substitute a true edifying love for the other and let God handle how that particular relationship will affect our future.

HOW TO FACE YOURSELF AGAIN

Our person-to-person work in healing may make life a little more difficult on the outside, but in the healing process, we will also face the hauntings of our own memory. Problems and criticism from without may find similar fears germinating within our minds. How can we really forget about our own errors and those of others? We may feel that even though we have tried to forget about what we did, we keep reliving it over and over again.

In the days after resolving our dispute, we can be tempted to doubt everything. We may wonder if people really believe us. We may wonder if we have done the right thing. We may doubt that someone has really forgiven us. We may question whether the other person will uphold his or her part of the agreement. That doubt is a direct assault on our faith.

Doubts can arise about every step we have taken. We may have second thoughts, after-the-fact worries, twenty-twenty hindsight. "If onlys" and "I should haves" are the germs that cause the decay of our faith. They keep us looking backward rather than forward—focused on our past rather than on the Cross.

It is important for us to remember our mistakes. Remembering is not constantly reliving the agony but remembering the positive things we have learned from them.

God's Memory: Teacher or Punisher?

God kept reminding His people about their faults so that they could learn from their past mistakes. His purpose was not to inflict repeated punishment; it was to keep them from making the same mistakes. The past, when properly remembered, made a better future.

Look how God waved Israel's sin in their faces: "Remember this and never forget how you provoked the LORD your God to anger in the desert. From the day you left Egypt until you arrived here, you have been rebellious against the LORD. At Horeb you aroused the LORD's wrath so that he was angry enough to destroy you" (Deut. 9:7–8).

Through Moses, God went on to deliver a long list of Israel's sins. The list, however, was not to browbeat the hearers but to encourage them to a better future of love and obedience to Him: "And now, O Israel, what does the LORD your God ask of you but to fear the LORD your God, to walk in all his ways, to love him, to serve the LORD your God with all your heart and with all your soul, and to observe the LORD's commands and decrees that I am giving you today for your own good?" (Deut. 10:12–13).

We must try to think about our past problems with a positive slant on the future. God allowed pain to occur and wants us to continue to benefit from its lessons. What can we learn?

Your Memory: Teacher or Punisher?

When we relive and rehash yesterday, we punish ourselves, and that is not constructive. Why are we going through the emotions all over again? When we decide to relive the bad past, we are usually down and depressed. In contrast, God wants us to remember the past and benefit from it. We have a choice when we review the past: we can view it as the world sees it, or we can view it as God sees it.

When we find ourselves remembering the conflict with pain or hostility, we may need to review the steps of forgiveness and reinforce the positive outcome of the resolution process. Are we reconciled to God and to ourselves? Have we made things right with the other person as far as it is possible?

Make the choice. Will we dwell on the past, which we cannot change, or will we live for the future, which we can and must have a responsible part in shaping? Are we going to punish ourselves forever or leave the past and move on? If we are going to move on, where is it we are going? Make a plan and follow it, with God's help.

Forgive and forget. Remember that forgetting does not mean putting it out of your mind. It means building a positive future on a negative past and that puts us right between the two—in the present.

The Power of the Present

Build on today, on what you have. The apostle John lays the foundation for what we have, "Dear friends, now we are children of God, and what we will be has not yet been made known" (1 John 3:2). What do we have? Just to mention one thing, we are children of God right now. John said that he did not know what we would turn out to be. It did not matter. The present has all we need.

What do we want from the future? There is one thing the future cannot do: Make us more of a child of God than we are right now. "*Now* we are children of God." Though the future holds many unknowns, we have all we need. The present cannot be better when we look at it this way. It is all we need for building a better future.

When we periodically mourn our social and personal losses from the conflict, we must make sure our grief is building toward a better future. Paul suggests that godly sorrow about our past mistakes can be a positive motivator: "Godly sorrow brings repentance that leads to salvation and leaves no regret, but worldly sorrow brings death. See what this godly sorrow has produced in you: what earnestness, what eagerness to clear yourselves, what indignation, what alarm, what longing, what concern, what readiness to see justice done. At every point you have proved yourselves to be innocent in this matter" (2 Cor. 7:10–11).

Godly sorrow lets us feel all the appropriate feelings, but it lets us move beyond them to maturity. It keeps us from repeating whatever our error was. That kind of sorrow does not brand us with an eternal scarlet letter of sin. It brands us with the white letter of purity in Christ.

End the Picking

How can the wounds heal if we keep picking at the scab? We must give it undisturbed time to heal. Stop the gossip. Stop the endless reevaluations and nitpicking. Stop the punishments and conditions. Exorcise the ghosts that haunt the mind and let the Holy Spirit work His miracle of healing. Step by step, from your heart to the hearts of others, He will heal our wounds.

Will we have scars? Yes, and those scars can be the positive reminders that our sin has been forgiven and that we are healed and renewed by the life of God in His scarred and risen Son.

PART III

MEDIATING THE CONFLICTS OF OTHERS

Like one who seizes a dog by the ears is a passer-by who meddles in a quarrel not his own (Proverbs 26:17).

CHAPTER 8
MEDIATING WITHOUT MEDDLING

So—you're ready to help others get their problems resolved? This chapter introduces you to the basic steps of more formal mediation. The effective mediator is (1) invited, (2) trustworthy, (3) sensitive, and (4) objective.

We are not the only ones with conflicts. We probably know a friend or two who could use some help in resolving disputes. Would you like to help? As we learn how to reconcile our own disputes, we will be able to help others do the same. We can be of help without becoming a full-time mediator or meddler. But before we get involved, we need to ask ourselves two questions: Can we be objective? Do people on both sides of the conflict want us to be involved?

Many disputes need the help of an impartial, third person. That could be us. Though many people would love to be used by God to make peace, most of them have not given conflict, resolution, and reconciliation enough thought to understand how they work. Solving our own problems is one thing, but working through the problems of others is quite a different matter. Though we will have to work harder on creating trust, listening, and not manipulating, the rewards of a peacemaker are great.

BEFORE YOU BEGIN

Helping to mediate a dispute puts us in a vulnerable position. It's a good idea to consider several questions first.

1. Do they want us involved? We should not begin to help our friends settle differences until they have invited us to help. But what if we see how we can help them but they haven't asked our help? First, we can suggest to them that an objective third person may be able to help them sort out the issues in the conflict. Then, we can offer to be that impartial person. Leave the offer at that point. Don't force yourself on them. Even if they respond with an invitation, be sure that it is genuine. Otherwise we will not have their trust. Always keep the attitude of a guest—involved in the problem at their invitation and only for as long as they want.

2. When is the best time to get involved? Try to get involved before the situation hits a crisis point. Prolonged frustration and previous defacing of each other leave emotional scars that become obstacles to trust. The best point to seek help is when people are aware they have a dispute and desire to settle it in an equitable and rational way.

3. Can we mediate without getting personally involved? We need to honestly examine our motives for becoming involved. Are we hoping that a successful resolution will make us look good? Are we satisfying our own ego needs? If we are, we have the wrong perspective on what we are doing as a mediator. If we take victory personally, we will soon come to take each aspect of the resolution process personally. We will have made the dispute our own and will soon need our own mediator.

As mediators, we must be sensitive to keep the decision making with those directly involved. That promotes a cooperative sharing of power, culminating in a transformed relationship.

GETTING STARTED

Before we actually begin the mediation process, we must make several choices.

1. Choose a method of mediation. What is the best way for us to help our friends? What are our options?

Shuttle diplomacy. One method is for us to meet with them individually to ascertain, confidentially of course, what they expect from the resolution and what they are willing to concede in order to reach an agreement. As a result of our observations, we may see a solution that could satisfy both sides. We may be able to negotiate a settlement that both are willing to accept. This procedure allows each party to adopt the solution as his or her own and avoids the danger that one will embrace it and the other will feel compelled to oppose it. It is effective where the people have feared that their concessions would be interpreted as signs of weakness.

Round-table negotiations. A second method is for us to meet with the parties jointly in order to assess the actual status of negotiations. Our goal will be to identify as explicitly as possible the real issues that resulted in impasse. The advantage of this approach is that we avoid being misled because each person will have to cover honestly the issues of the disagreement. A second advantage of this procedure is that we may be able to obtain agreement from both sides on the phrasing of the issues.

Joint and private. A third method, practiced more than the others, is a combination of separate and joint meetings to facilitate agreement between the people. In this approach the people are usually first brought together to clarify the issues. Then, in private meetings, we can receive confidential and privileged communications from each person. We can work back and forth between the people as a channel of communication until we sense agreement or a need to bring them together again.

2. Consider a formal agreement. If we are invited to help resolve a large-scale dispute, like a church split, a deadlocked business partnership, or potential divorce, we might want to begin with a formal agreement that states the willingness of those involved to negotiate and reconcile. It should outline the issues. The people should carefully review the agreement and make sure that they agree with its terms. It should state that all agree to settle their dispute according to biblical principles.

AS WE PROCEED

Great—now the negotiations are underway. But they're likely to fall flat unless we and the participants in the dispute can operate according to several principles as we proceed.

1. Remember to seek the Lord's help. Before we begin each meeting, we may want to outline some of the dynamics of the conflict that need the Lord's healing touch: unforgiveness, pride, jealousy, fear, or anxiety. Then pray together, remembering both to praise the Lord for who He is and to intercede for one another. After praying, we can discuss the purpose of the meeting. Emphasize that the ultimate purpose of the meeting is to reconcile both sides to each other through the resolution of their dispute. Apply Scripture appropriately.

2. Provide guidance, not a verdict. We need to be careful to let the two sides explore and seek resolution for their differences. We have no authority to impose the final solution. Our strength lies in the ability to assist our friends in resolving their differences. The dispute is settled when they themselves reach what they consider to be a workable solution.

We may find that we need to guide uncontrolled emotions. If the disputing people lose control of their emotions, they will hurt each other and seriously impede the process. If you feel tempers flaring, suggest to the people that their anger could jeopardize the negotiations. Remind them that they have committed themselves to a fair and just resolution. Whenever emotions supplant reasoning, agreement is impossible. All too often when emotions are high, people in the heat of the argument may take a final position prematurely. Having done so, it may be difficult for them to retreat from it when a later proposal is advanced.

3. Make each step clear. Make sure both sides know what is happening. We will have to use the listening and communicating skills outlined in chapter six. Knowing what is going on avoids hard feelings later when one or the other might feel that an assumed rule has been violated or when someone just flatly dislikes how the mediation is being handled.

4. Respect confidences. Trust is critical in mediation. It is essential that all parties have complete confidence in our integrity and ability. If they come to doubt our impartiality or ability, we should walk away. Our friends have enough problems without having to cope with their distrust of us.

Trust is established by behaving consistently and predictably and by never violating a confidence. We will hear a lot of personal facts about our friends. It must be understood that all information we receive is confidential. We must make sure that everyone understands that disclosure of any oral or written information can only happen by approval of everyone involved.

5. Keep positions and procedures straight. We will have to think on two levels at the same time. We have to become clear about not only the positions of each party but also the issues that led to impasse. Then we have to ask questions about the mediation process itself. Are we sensitive to what the people are saying, or did we miss an important point? Do we know what the central issue is? Are we jumping around from issue to issue? Did someone change the subject, leaving the last point in limbo? Should we challenge whether or not the new subject is relevant to the issues under discussion?

We may find it helpful to leave one issue and move on to

another. That may happen before or after an issue has been fully clarified. Sometimes the people become so deadlocked that agreement is unlikely. They may then agree to disagree and to take up another issue related to the general topic. We may also discover a hidden issue that must be settled before the issue under mediation can be explored productively.

6. Try to maintain a balance of power. One of our goals is to help avoid a win-lose struggle, where each side tries to force the other to its own position. We can work to make sure that a relative balance of power exists between both sides. The ability of each party to exercise some sanction over the other is necessary to ensure that all parties will enter into the negotiation process with good faith. Watch out for other various styles of disputing discussed in chapter three.

7. Be a reality reflector. People in the middle of a dispute usually have a distorted and imbalanced perspective of reality. As mediators, we can reflect a more realistic picture for our friends. We can look at the dispute with a fresh and impartial perspective. When disputants get bogged down in little things they've blown out of proportion, an effective mediator stops the discussion and tries to bring it back to more realistic and pertinent issues.

When our friends begin to condemn and judge each other by magnifying the severity and consequence of the offense, we can try to sum up its actual weight and scope in an unbiased manner. Then the issue can become an objective question of fact, not a personal slur.

When the parties show a misunderstanding of the facts, leading to further conflict and accusations, you as mediator must understand all the relevant facts and communicate that understanding. Ask the parties if they agree or disagree with those facts. That not only aids in establishing open and reality-based communication; it also discourages further misunderstandings in the interpretation of the facts.

It is important for us to accurately reflect the position of both sides. We should discuss any potential areas of concession. If there are none, we will need to meet individually with each person. In those private sessions we should maintain complete objectivity as we reflect both sides. We can point out the weaknesses and the strengths of each party's position. We can express our feelings about the areas of disagreement, and we can recommend possible areas of compromise. But we must not take sides and end up participating in the conflict.

8. Introduce new ideas. A great part of our help relates to exploring new ideas. The people involved may have ideas that they will share with us but not with each other; they may be afraid of looking too ready to give in. We can offer the ideas in a more objective way, letting each person then accept or reject them without any loss of face. If the suggestion is acceptable, then it can become an offer.

Attempt to stimulate counterproposals, compromises, and concessions by infusing new ideas, by suggesting new combinations of compromises, and by serving as a fresh vehicle for communication about delicate points.

9. Look for resolution. We must listen carefully to what is being said. Can we detect an area of potential agreement that should be explored? We must be alert to any sign of willingness to compromise. We can even suggest the basis for such compromise.

If the dispute is not resolved after a reasonable time, we can review the discussion. We must be careful not to express any judgmental attitude or any preference of one position over the other. We must merely review what has taken place in the past and discuss any areas that have interfered with the settlement discussion.

Our work with others should follow the same procedure outlined throughout this book. The major difference is making certain that we are welcome and that we do not play favorites. Beyond that, we will have to wait on the Holy Spirit to help our friends humble themselves to the reconciling forgiveness of God.

Be kind and compassionate to one
another, forgiving each other,
just as in Christ God forgave you
(Ephesians 4:32).

CHAPTER 9
WE CAN WORK MIRACLES

*Problems have been resolved; people have
been reconciled; words of hate have turned
to acts of love—surely this is a miracle of
God's own forgiveness.*

THE MIRACLE OF FORGIVENESS

Satan and all his forces were against God's work of forgiveness in Christ. Satan tried to derail Christ from His mission of forgiveness. The devil detests forgiveness and those who forgive. He blinds people's eyes so that they will not see the light of God's forgiveness in the gospel. He also hardens the hearts of those who have believed. He would like to dry up every drop of compassionate forgiveness in our bodies. His power is strong.

We are not naïve. We know that to forgive is to ask for an ongoing miracle of God in our lives. Each forgiving act has the powers of hell against it and the power of heaven above it. How is there ever a completed act of forgiveness except by the miraculous power of the Holy Spirit?

We should never fool ourselves into thinking that if we merely follow the five steps to reconciliation, everything will turn out fine. We could, on our own, follow the external steps, but it takes the power of God to make us really believe and be forgiving on the inside where only He sees. This book asks you to trust God and witness a miracle: forgiveness.

THE MIRACLE OF RESOLUTION AND HEALING

This has also been a book about resolution. To forgive someone is a miracle of grace that requires yet another wonder—the resolution of the conflict. To resolve a dispute takes a miracle of humility and perseverance. To resolve a dispute is to cease manipulation and to trust a sovereign God.

When the trauma of conflict subsides, the most beautiful miracle of all begins to unfold. The weapons of hostility are beaten into the instruments of peace. Enemies turn to friends.

Words of hate turn to acts of love. The miracle of reconciliation flowers.

This has been a book about how we can know the healing power of God through conflict and reconciliation. To many people the Cross is a sign of humiliation, losing, and a dead-end future. To the eyes of faith it is the doorway to the experience of forgiveness and life with God. Conflict to many is a destructive and shameful experience that ruins an hour, a day, or a life. To the eyes of faith it is the doorway to solving problems, healing wounds, and a future full of the grace of God.

We are not saying these kind of miracles come easily or without pain. They come through sadness and brokenness. Miracles happen when the depths of our own darkness is flooded by the brilliance of God's grace in Christ. Miracles are forged on the mundane anvil of working out problems point by point with other mortals. Above all, miracles are not of human origin. These miracles come from God the Father and are sent through His exalted Son.

SUMMARY OF THE STEPS TO RESOLUTION AND RECONCILIATION

1. Understand what we're really after when we argue (chapter 3)
2. Resolve our conflicts with God (chapter 4)
   a. Admit that we are part of the problem (pp. 50–52)
   b. Avoid punishing others and excusing ourselves (pp. 52–54)
   c. Avoid retaliating with anger (pp. 54–57)
   d. Give our problems to God (pp. 58–61)
   e. A crisis checklist (pp. 61–62)
3. Resolve our conflicts with ourselves (chapter 5)
   a. Learn to appreciate our forgiveness (pp. 64–72)
   b. What if we don't *feel* forgiven? (pp. 72–74)
4. Resolve our conflicts with the other person (chapter 6)
   a. Arrange the first meeting (pp. 78–80)
   b. Four steps to setting a positive tone (pp. 80–83)
   c. Five keys to resolving a problem (pp. 83–95)
5. Allow time for healing (chapter 7)
   a. Distinguish between resolution and reconciliation (pp. 98–99)
   b. Deal with minds that never forget (pp. 99–103)
   c. How to face people again (pp. 104–107)
   d. How to face yourself again (pp. 107–110)

756 37

DATE DUE

MEDIATION AGREEMENT

_____ and _____
(Party A)   (Party B)

hereby agree to have their dispute(s) settled by mediation. The dispute(s) are:

_____

_____

_____

_____

_____

_____

_____

It is the desire of each person that this dispute be resolved in accord with biblical principles.

The parties agree that _____ shall act as mediator to resolve the dispute between them.

In witness hereof, the parties have signed this agreement this _____ day of _____, 19____.

Signed: _____

_____

Witness: _____

_____